W0090823

Contents

JONES & BARTLETT LEARNING INFORMATION SYSTEMS SECURITY & ASSURANCE SERIES

LABORATORY MANUAL TO ACCOMPANY

Security Strategies in Web Applications and Social Networking

1E REVISED

JONES & BARTLETT
LEARNING

World Headquarters
Jones & Bartlett Learning
5 Wall Street
Burlington, MA 01803
978-443-5000
info@jblearning.com
www.jblearning.com

Jones & Bartlett Learning books and products are available through most bookstores and online booksellers. To contact Jones & Bartlett Learning directly, call 800-832-0034, fax 978-443-8000, or visit our website, www.jblearning.com.

Substantial discounts on bulk quantities of Jones & Bartlett Learning publications are available to corporations, professional associations, and other qualified organizations. For details and specific discount information, contact the special sales department at Jones & Bartlett Learning via the above contact information or send an email to specialsales@jblearning.com.

Production Credits
Chief Executive Officer: Ty Field
President: James Homer
SVP, Editor-in-Chief: Michael Johnson
SVP, Chief Marketing Officer: Alison M. Pendergast
SVP, Curriculum Solutions: Christopher Will
Director of Sales, Curriculum Solutions: Randi Roger
Author: vLab Solutions, LLC, David Kim, President
Editorial Management: High Stakes Writing, LLC, Lawrence J. Goodrich,
    Editor and Publisher
Copy editor, High Stakes Writing: Katherine Dillin
Senior Editorial Assistant: Rainna Erikson

Reprints and Special Projects Manager: Susan Schultz
Production Editor: Tina Chen
Rights & Photo Research Associate: Lian Bruno
Manufacturing and Inventory Control Supervisor: Amy Bacus
Senior Marketing Manager: Andrea DeFronzo
Cover Design: Anne Spencer
Composition: CAE Solutions Corp.
Cover Image: © ErickN/ShutterStock, Inc.
Printing and Binding: Edwards Brothers Malloy
Cover Printing: Edwards Brothers Malloy

ISBN: 978-1-4496-3859-7

6048
Printed in the United States of America
16 15 14 13 12   10 9 8 7 6 5 4 3 2

Ethics and Code of Conduct

The material presented in this course is designed to give you a real-life look at the use of various tools and systems that are at the heart of every network security analyst's daily responsibilities. Through use of this material, you will have access to software and techniques used every day by professionals. With this access come certain ethical responsibilities.

The hardware, software, tools, and applications presented and used in this lab manual and/or the VSCL are intended to be used for instructional and educational purposes only.

As a student in this course, you are not to use these tools, applications, or techniques on live production IT infrastructures inside or outside of your campus or organization. Under no circumstances are you permitted to use these tools, applications, or techniques on the production IT infrastructures and networks of other organizations.

You are required to conform to your school or organization's Code of Conduct and ethics policies during the use of this lab manual and any of the tools, applications, or techniques described within.

Preface

Welcome! This lab manual is your step-by-step guide to completing the laboratory exercises for this course.

Virtual Security Cloud Lab (VSCL)

For some of the exercises in this lab manual, you will use the Virtual Security Cloud Lab (VSCL) resource.

Note:

The Virtual Security Cloud Lab requires use of either **Windows Internet Explorer** or **Mozilla Firefox**. The Virtual Security Cloud Lab does not support Google Chrome, Safari, or Opera at this time.

The VSCL is a collection of virtual resources, including Windows and Linux servers, Cisco routers, and applications such as Wireshark, FileZilla, and Nessus®, that will allow you to perform all of the tasks in this lab manual as if you were performing them in a live production environment. The heart of the VSCL is a Windows Workstation desktop configured to give you access to the tools and resources you need for each lab, without any special setup on your part.

As noted in the following table, some of the exercises in this lab manual will be performed without using the VSCL. For detailed instructions on how to perform these exercises, please consult your syllabus or instructor.

How to Use This Lab Manual

This lab manual features step-by-step instructions for completing the following hands-on lab exercises:

VSCL	LAB TITLE
Yes	Lab #1: Evaluate Business World Transformation: The Impact of the Internet and WWW
No	Lab #2: Engage in Internet Research to Obtain Useful Personal Information
Yes	Lab #3: Perform a Post-Mortem Review of a Data Breach Incident
Yes	Lab #4: Exploit Known Web Vulnerabilities on a Live Web Server
No	Lab #5: Apply OWASP to a Web Security Assessment
No	Lab #6: Align Compliance Requirements to HIPAA, FISMA, GLBA, SOX, PCI DSS, and AICPA
Yes	Lab #7: Perform Dynamic and Static Quality Control Testing
No	Lab #8: Perform an IT and Web Application Security Assessment
No	Lab #9: Recognize Risks and Threats Associated with Social Networking and Mobile Communications
No	Lab #10: Build a Web Application and Security Development Life Cycle Plan

Video Walkthroughs of Each Lab

Each VSCL-based exercise in this lab manual includes a video walkthrough that gives you a quick overview of every step and function. You can watch the video walkthrough prior to performing the lab exercise, and refer to it as necessary while you complete the lab. You can pause, rewind, and fast-forward the video walkthroughs if you need to take notes or spend extra time on a particular step or function. Consult your syllabus or instructor for information on where to locate the walkthrough videos.

Step-by-Step Instructions

You'll find it easy to complete these lab exercises by following the detailed step-by-step instructions. Each step is clearly broken down into sub-steps, and all actions you are required to take are noted in **bold** font. Screenshots are included to help you identify key menus, dialog boxes, and input locations. If you get stuck on a step, refer to the lab video, which follows the order of the steps.

Deliverables

At the completion of each lab, you'll be asked to provide a set of deliverables to your instructor. These deliverables may include documents, files, screenshots, and/or answers to assessment questions. The deliverables are designed to test your understanding of the information, and your successful completion of the steps and functions of the lab. For specific information on deliverables, refer to the **Deliverables** section at the end of each lab.

 Note:

Some labs require the use of a word processor such as Microsoft® Word for preparing and submitting deliverables. If you do not have access to a word processor, you can use OpenOffice on the Workstation desktop of the VSCL to prepare your documents. It includes a word processor called Writer that has all the features necessary for creating documents for use in these labs.

File Transfer

At times, you may be asked to transfer to another computer files you have created while performing lab steps in the VSCL. This can be performed using the File Transfer function built in to the vWorkstation desktop of the VSCL. Instructions for preparing and sending files using the File Transfer function can be found at the beginning of the video walkthrough for the first lab in each course (in most cases, Lab #1).

 Note:

Use of this lab manual or the VSCL **does not require use of the textbook**. If you have questions about whether a textbook is needed for your course, consult your instructor.

Evaluate Business World Transformation: The Impact of the Internet and WWW

Introduction

Connecting to the Internet is like advertising to the world where you are and which data you may have behind your website. Attackers, perpetrators, and cyber-criminals seek to compromise and access systems, applications, databases, and confidential information. In this lab, you will learn the realities of connecting to the Internet and the World Wide Web (WWW). You will ensure that several readily available utilities for determining the vulnerability of Web-based applications are properly installed on the lab's Web server. You will also complete a business impact analysis for several real-world situations.

Learning Objectives

Upon completing this lab, you will be able to:

- Identify security challenges on the Web as they relate to various business models and determine the impact they have on e-commerce and Internet-based deployments
- Distinguish among the different reasons for attacks on websites and determine exactly what attackers are after when they target a WWW presence
- Evaluate the current state of security on a LAMP server using SSH, skipfish, and tcpdump to identify whether the proper tools are installed for evaluating the security of the server
- Install and use the Firefox Web browser with the Live HTTP Headers plug-in

TOOLS AND SOFTWARE	
NAME	**MORE INFORMATION**
Damn Vulnerable Web Application (DVWA)	http://www.dvwa.co.uk/
PuTTY	http://www.chiark.greenend.org.uk/~sgtatham/putty/
skipfish	http://code.google.com/p/skipfish/
tcpdump	http://www.tcpdump.org/

Deliverables

Upon completion of this lab, you are required to provide the following deliverables to your instructor:

1. Compromised Business Impact Analysis;
2. Lab Assessment Questions & Answers for Lab #1.

Hands-On Steps

1. This lab begins at the student landing vWorkstation virtual machine desktop of the VSCL, as shown here.

FIGURE 1.1

"Student Landing" VSCL
workstation

> **Note:**
> The next steps will use SSH to connect to the lab's Web server, TargetUbuntu01, and verify that skipfish and tcpdump are properly installed.

2. **Double-click** the **PuTTY icon** on the desktop to open the PuTTY application.

   PuTTY is a free utility that can open secure remote connections over the Internet via Telnet or SSH (secure shell).

3. In the PuTTY application window, **type** the IP address for the TargetUbuntu01 server, **172.30.0.4**. **Select** the **SSH radio button** and **click** the **Open button** to start the connection.

FIGURE 1.2

Using PuTTY to connect
to TargetUbuntu01

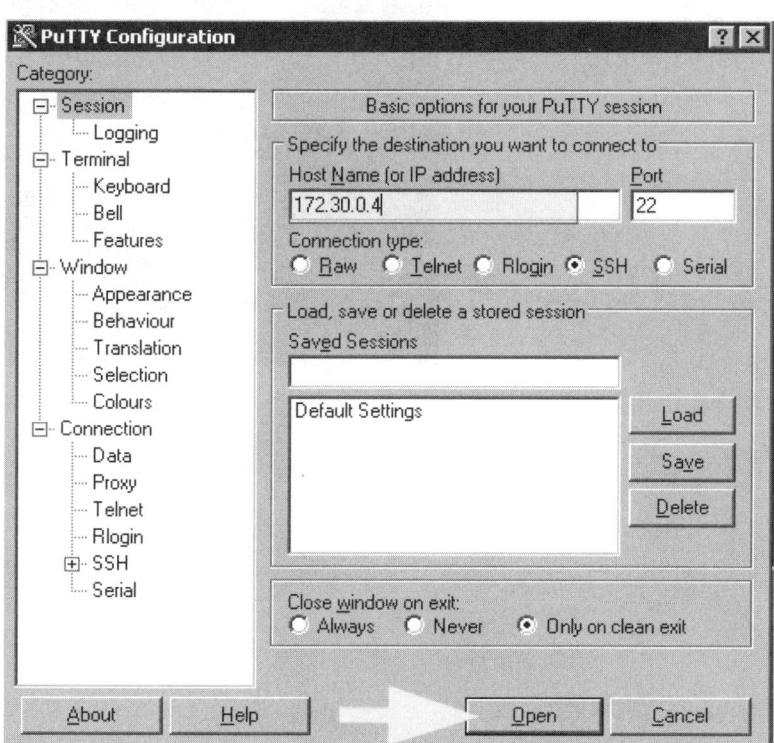

4. PuTTY will launch a terminal console window. At the login prompt, **type** the following credentials:
   - Username: **student**
   - Password: **ISS316Security**

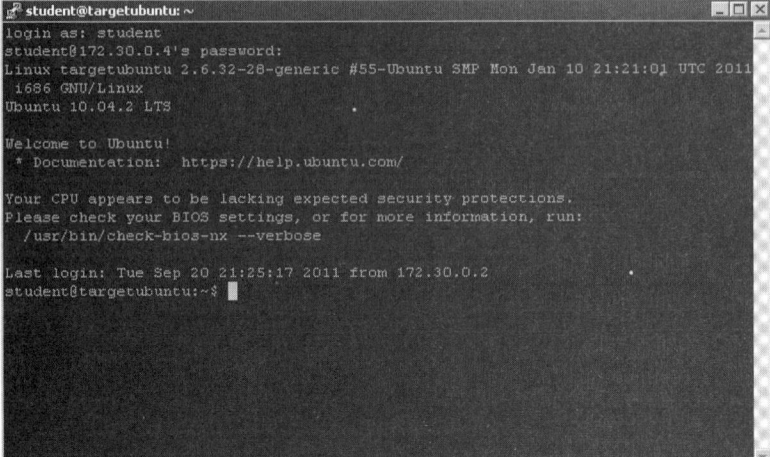

5. At the command prompt, **type ifconfig –a** and **press Enter** to verify the IP address for the server.

   The IP address is displayed after the abbreviation *inet addr* in the eth0 section of the results. eth0 is
   the interface used to access TargetUbuntu01. This IP address should match the one you entered in
   the PuTTY application window.

6. At the command prompt, **type tcpdump –h** and **press Enter** to verify that tcpdump is installed on this server.

   Tcpdump is a command line packet analyzer.

FIGURE 1.5

Verifying tcpdump is installed

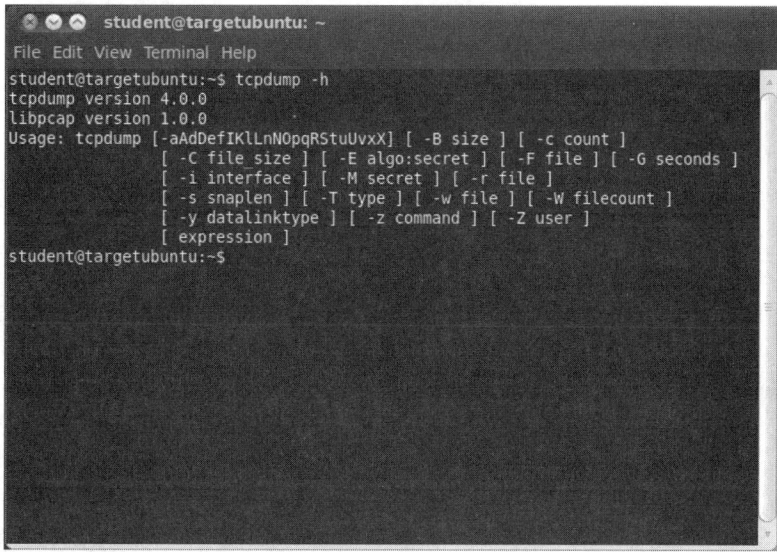

7. **Record** the **tcpdump version number** that appears on the screen: _____.
8. **Record** the **tcpdump usage message** that appears on the screen: _____.
9. At the command prompt, **type skipfish –h** and **press Enter** to verify that skipfish is installed on this server.

   Skipfish is a utility that crawls through Web applications and provides a map of possible security leaks for later assessment.

FIGURE 1.6

Viewing the skipfish onscreen manual

This screen displays all of the command line options for the tool and descriptions for each. Use the arrow keys to scroll through the manual to learn more about this tool. **Press CTRL** and **type Z** to return to the command line prompt.

10. **Minimize** the **terminal window**.

 Note:
The next steps will use the Firefox browser to access the Damn Vulnerable Web Application (DVWA) and select the Live HTTP Headers plug-in for the Firefox browser.

---

11. **Double-click** the **Mozilla Firefox icon** on the desktop to open the Firefox browser.

    You can access the DVWA tool using any Internet browser, but the steps in this lab will use the Firefox browser.

12. In the browser's address box, **type http://172.30.0.4/dvwa** and **press Enter** to open the Damn Vulnerable Web Application.

    DVWA is a Web application that is made purposefully vulnerable. It is installed on a local Web server to allow security analysts a safe place to test the security of their applications.

FIGURE 1.7

DVWA login screen

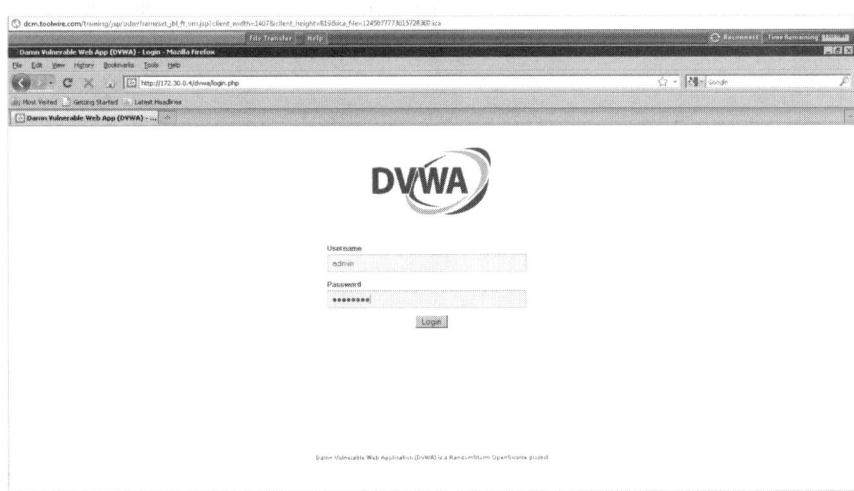

13. **Log in** to the application with the following credentials and **click Login** to continue:
    - Username: **admin**
    - Password: **password**
14. **Review** the **navigation buttons** on the left-hand side of the page to become familiar with the tools available on the DVWA.

15. In the Firefox browser's toolbar, **click Tools** and then **click Live HTTP headers** in the menu to turn on this option.

    The Live HTTP headers add-on allows the user to view the HTTP header of any page viewed in the Firefox browser.

FIGURE 1.8

Live HTTP headers option on the Firefox browser

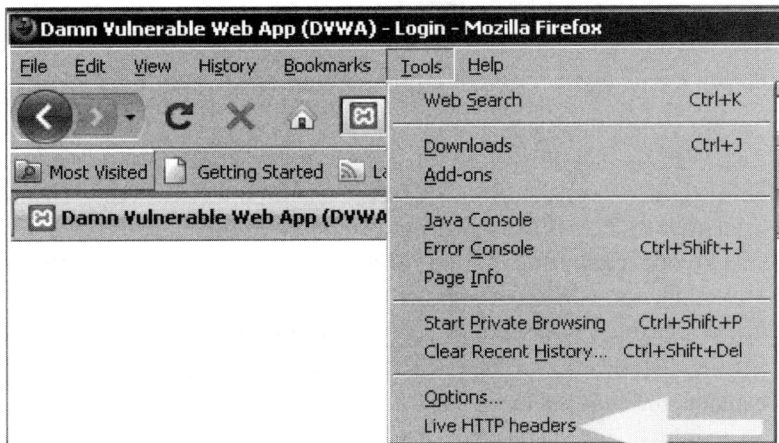

16. **Minimize** the **Live HTTP headers dialog box**.
17. **Click** the **Reload current page icon** on the Firefox toolbar to refresh the page.
18. **Maximize** the **Live HTTP headers dialog box**.

    The dialog box will display the HTML code for the header of the active Web page, in this case, the DVWA application.

FIGURE 1.9

Live HTTP headers dialog box

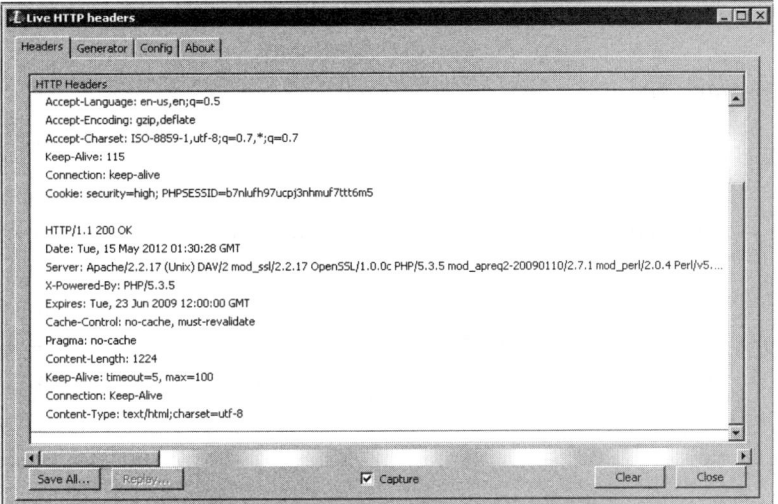

19. **Close** the **Live HTTP headers dialog box**.
20. **Close** the **Firefox browser**.

> **Note:**
> The next steps will use your understanding of the vulnerabilities of Web applications to access the business threats inherent in each of the scenarios presented below and submit them in a Compromised Business Impact Analysis document as a deliverable for this lab.

21. **Create** a new text document entitled **Compromised Business Impact Analysis Lab #1**.

22. **Review** the following scenario:

    As a Web Applications security specialist, you know that Internet threats go well beyond an attacker defacing your website. An attack can also include extracting customers' privacy data or confidential information. This is a major threat not only to the organization but to the customers as well. In fact, 70 percent of all unauthorized access and loss of data comes from Internet-based attacks on websites and applications where users are on the World Wide Web (WWW). Your immediate supervisor has asked for your assessment of each of the following situations.

23. In your text document, **describe** the business threats posed by each of the following situations and **explain** what its effect may be if a Web application is compromised:

    - A publicly traded retailer with retail outlets and online shopping/shipping
    - A small, private law firm's website with forms for potential clients to complete, including name, address, contact number, and reason for scheduling an appointment
    - A real estate appraisal company that provides online appraisals for a publicly traded financial institution's residential-loan applicants. The bank sends all applicant information to the appraisal company electronically
    - A Web-hosting company that provides leased servers for websites of clients ranging from small firms to large online retailers
    - A city government that allows people with parking tickets to pay the fines online using a credit card or online check
    - A local residential-cleaning business with a website that acts as a company brochure; no forms of any type are located on the website
    - A software development company that develops and licenses online shopping software to large corporations
    - A private, locally owned bank with a website that accepts loan applications online
    - A local doctor's office that keeps all patient information at the office, doesn't share electronically with any entities, and doesn't have a website or use any custom-developed software
    - An online-only retailer that sells athletic equipment using shopping-cart software that has been developed in-house and uses PayPal whenever a customer makes a purchase

24. **Submit** the **text document** to your instructor as a deliverable for this lab.

Evaluation Criteria and Rubrics

The following are the evaluation criteria and rubrics for Lab #1 that students must perform:

1. Was the student able to identify security challenges on the Web as they relate to various business models and determine the impact they have on e-commerce and Internet-based deployments? – [**25%**]

2. Was the student able to distinguish among the different reasons for attacks on websites and determine exactly what attackers are after when they target a WWW presence? – [**25%**]

3. Was the student able to evaluate the current state of security on a LAMP server using SSH, skipfish, and tcpdump to identify whether the proper tools are installed for evaluating the security of the server? – [**25%**]

4. Was the student able to install and use the Firefox Web browser with the Live HTTP Headers plug-in? – [**25%**]

LAB #1 – ASSESSMENT WORKSHEET

Evaluate Business World Transformation: The Impact of the Internet and WWW

Course Name and Number:
_____

Student Name:
_____

Instructor Name:
_____

Lab Due Date:
_____

Overview

Connecting to the Internet is like advertising to the world where you are and which data you may have behind your website. Attackers, perpetrators, and cyber-criminals seek to compromise and access systems, applications, databases, and confidential information. In this lab, you learned the realities of connecting to the Internet and the World Wide Web (WWW). You ensured that several readily available utilities for determining the vulnerability of Web-based applications are properly installed on the lab's Web server. You also completed a business impact analysis for several real-world situations.

Lab Assessment Questions & Answers

1. From the results of the Compromised Business Impact Analysis, what do you consider to be the greatest type of risk and why?

   _____

   _____

   _____

   _____

2. Why is it critical to perform periodic Web-application vulnerability assessments and penetration tests?

   _____

   _____

   _____

   _____

3. What kind of Web application does Damn Vulnerable Web Application (DVWA) use?

_____

_____

_____

_____

4. Why is connecting your Web servers and Web applications to the Internet like opening Pandora's box?

_____

_____

_____

_____

5. What does the skipfish application do, and why is it a good security tool for Web servers and Web-application testing?

_____

_____

_____

_____

_____

_____

_____

_____

6. What is tcpdump, and why is it a good tool for testing the Ubuntu Linux Web server and Web-application security?

_____

_____

_____

_____

7. What does the Firefox Live HTTP Headers plug-in application do, and why is this a good tool for Web-server and Web-application security testing?

_____

_____

_____

_____

_____

_____

_____

_____

8. What does using the -h switch for tcpdump and skipfish do?

_____

_____

_____

9. What is a major difference between typing commands and file names on Linux and in Windows?

_____

_____

_____

_____

10. Why is Telnet not recommended for remote access to a Web server? What do you recommend and why?

_____

_____

_____

_____

Engage in Internet Research to Obtain Useful Personal Information

Introduction

Many people do not realize how much personal information and data can be found about them on the Internet. In this lab, you will explore a variety of search engines and social networking websites that may contain personal information about you that, in the hands of a hacker, could compromise and exploit your privacy. You will document the sites that display your personal information and suggest methods for controlling access to that information within the specific sites.

This lab is a paper-based design lab and does not require use of the Virtual Security Cloud Lab (VSCL). To successfully complete the deliverables for this lab, you will need access to a text editor or word processor, such as Microsoft® Word. For some labs, you may also need access to a graphics line drawing application, such as Visio or PowerPoint.

> **Note:**
> If you don't have a word processor or graphics package, use OpenOffice on the student landing vWorkstation for your lab deliverables and to answer the lab assessment questions. To capture screenshots, **press Prt Sc > MSPAINT, paste** into a text document, and **save** the document in the Security_Strategies folder (**C:\Security_ Strategies**) using the File Transfer function.

Learning Objectives

Upon completing this lab, you will be able to:

- Use Internet search engines to obtain publicly available personal identifiable information (PII) similar to the way attackers do
- Facilitate social-networking sites to obtain PII from targets, similar to the way attackers would use publicly available information to infer and deduce valuable PII
- Recognize the availability and services of websites that provide publicly available personal information for a nominal fee or free
- Capture the information that is available from government websites as "publicly available" but that may be sensitive and reveal personal information
- Identify ways attackers can use information provided by an organization's website to perform social-engineering attacks on its employees

TOOLS AND SOFTWARE	
NAME	**MORE INFORMATION**
None	

Deliverables

Upon completion of this lab, you are required to provide the following deliverables to your instructor:

1. Personal Information Research Report Lab #2;
2. Lab Assessment Questions & Answers for Lab #2.

Hands-On Steps

1. This lab begins at a workstation with Internet access. **Double-click** any **Internet browser icon** on your desktop to open the application.

> **Note:**
> The next steps will explore various Internet search engines to see what personal information about you is readily available.

2. In a new text document, **create** a **Personal Information Research Report Lab** #2.

    You will be responsible for determining what to document in this report based on your evaluation of the results of the Internet searches you perform in this lab.

3. For each of the Internet searches in the steps below, include the following items in your text document:
    *   **Make a screen capture** of any sites that displayed more personal information than you expected to find on that site
    *   **Describe** how the actual results differed from your expectations
    *   **Explain** what steps you might take to limit how much of your personal information is available on the Internet

4. In your browser's address box, **type dogpile.com** to open the search tool.

5. In the search box, **type *your name*** replacing the generic *your name* with your actual name and **press** the **Go Fetch button**.

6. **Click at least two** of the search results that appear to refer to your personal information and review the data available.

7. In your browser's address box, **type google.com** to open the search tool.

8. In the search box, **type *your e-mail address*** replacing the generic *your e-mail address* with your actual e-mail address and **press** the **Search button**.

9. **Click at least two** of the search results that appear to refer to your personal information and review the data available.

10. In your browser's address box, **type intelius.com** to open the search tool.

11. In the search box, **type *your name*** and ***your state*** in the relevant fields and **press** the **Search button**.

12. **Click** the **Get the Report on button** for the search result that appears to refer to your personal information and review the data available for sale.

13. In your browser's address box, **type alltheinternet.com** to open the search tool.

14. **Click** the **Advanced Search link** to the right of the Search button.

15. In the **Find results with all of the words** box, **type *your name*** replacing the generic *your name* with your actual name and **press** the **Search button**.

16. In the **Find results with at least one of the words** box, **type *keywords*** replacing the generic *keywords* with at least two words that describe hobbies or sports or other activities that you associate with yourself and **press** the **Advanced Search button**.

17. **Click at least two** of the search results that appear to refer to your personal information and review the data available.

18. In your browser's address box, **type people.yahoo.com** to open the search tool.

19. In the relevant search boxes, **type *your first name*** and ***your last name*** and **press** the **Search button**.

20. **Click at least two** of the search results that appear to refer to your personal information and review the data available.

21. In your browser's address box, **type peoplesearch.com** to open the search tool.
22. In the relevant search boxes, **type *your first name* and *your last name* and *your state*** and **press the Find button**.
23. **Click at least two** of the search results that appear to refer to your personal information and review the data available.
24. In your browser's address box, **type zabasearch.com** to open the search tool.
25. In the **Search by phone number** box, **type *your phone number*** replacing the generic *your phone number* with your actual phone number and **press the Find button**.
26. In your browser's address box, **type dogpile.com** to open the search tool.
27. In the search box, **type *your county* and *your state*** replacing the generic *your county* and *your state* with your actual information and **press the Go Fetch button**.
28. **Click** the **link** for your county's official site to open the site.
29. **Review** the search options on the government site and see what information can be obtained by searching for your name.
30. In your browser's address box, **type google.com** to open the search tool.
31. In the search box, **type how to find personal information** and **press the Search button**.
32. **Click at least two** of the search results to see how easily publicly available information can be purchased.
33. **Close** the **browser window**.
34. **Submit** the **text document** to your instructor as a deliverable for this lab.

Evaluation Criteria and Rubrics

The following are the evaluation criteria and rubrics for Lab #2 that students must perform:

1. Was the student able to use Internet search engines to obtain publicly available personal identifiable information (PII) similar to the way attackers do? – **[20%]**
2. Was the student able to facilitate social-networking sites to obtain PII from targets, similar to the way attackers would use publicly available information to infer and deduce valuable PII? – **[20%]**
3. Was the student able to recognize the availability and services of websites that provide publicly available personal information for a nominal fee or free? – **[20%]**
4. Was the student able to capture the information that is available from government websites as "publicly available" but that may be sensitive and reveal personal information? – **[20%]**
5. Was the student able to identify ways attackers can use information provided by an organization's website to perform social-engineering attacks on its employees? – **[20%]**

LAB #2 – ASSESSMENT WORKSHEET

Engage in Internet Research to Obtain Useful Personal Information

Course Name and Number:

Student Name:

Instructor Name:

Lab Due Date:

Overview

Many people do not realize how much personal information and data can be found about them on the Internet. In this lab, you explored a variety of search engines and social-networking websites that may contain personal information about you that, in the hands of a hacker, could compromise and exploit your privacy. You documented the sites that displayed your personal information and suggested methods for controlling access to that information within the specific sites.

Lab Assessment Questions & Answers

1. How does dogpile.com expose personal information that can be found on the World Wide Web?

2. Complete the following table as it relates to finding personal information about yourself on the Internet:

METHOD	WAS PERSONAL INFORMATION RETURNED? (YES OR NO)
"Your name" in dogpile.com	
"Your e-mail address" in google.com	
"Your name" and *"your state"* in intelius.com	
"Your name" in alltheinternet.com with various keywords	
"Your name" in a Yahoo People search	
"Your name" in Peoplesearch.com	
"Your phone number" in zabasearch.com	
"Your name" in a government website for the county you live in	

3. Was there enough personal information returned that could potentially be used for identity theft? Explain why or why not.

_____

_____

_____

_____

4. What is the security implication of having a webmail account compromised as it pertains to a social-networking website?

_____

_____

_____

_____

5. How can identity thieves take advantage of other Facebook users and steal personal information?

_____

_____

_____

_____

6. According to Facebook.com, who owns the information posted by a user?

_____

_____

_____

_____

_____

_____

_____

_____

_____

_____

_____

_____

7. Where within Facebook.com can you, as a user, define what is private and what is public-domain information with your profile information?

_____

_____

_____

_____

8. What is a security feature you should always look for in any website that will ask for personal information to share with others?

_____

_____

_____

_____

9. What implications can the social-networking sites have for job applicants?

_____

_____

_____

_____

10. What is the risk of combining your family and personal friends with your business contacts and associates?

_____

_____

_____

_____

11. What type of personal information could an attacker obtain from a user profile on LinkedIn.com that he or she could use for identity theft?

_____

_____

_____

_____

12. Suppose someone posted your highly confidential personal information on a social-networking site, and you wish to have the results removed from the Google search engine. Describe some actions you could take to have the information removed.

_____

_____

_____

_____

13. How does one find publicly available records online?

_____

_____

_____

_____

14. Suppose you find your "tweets" from twitter.com reveal too much personal information. What are some options if you wish to continue "tweeting," yet protect the information from public view?

_____

_____

_____

_____

15. List the type of information you can obtain from a reverse telephone lookup on sites such as zabasearch.com.

_____

_____

_____

_____

Perform a Post-Mortem Review of a Data Breach Incident

Introduction

In this lab, you will perform a live brute force attack on the TargetUbuntu01 Web server and configure tcpdump to capture traffic on the Web server while the brute force attack is occurring. You also will dissect HTTP header information to determine desirable and undesirable session types and use Webalizer, a Web analysis tool, to investigate statistics gathered from Web logs. Finally, you will explore how Google analytics and Yahoo! analytics can be used for search-engine optimization.

Learning Objectives

Upon completing this lab, you will be able to:

- Analyze Web traffic in real time using tcpdump to capture traffic as it happens on the network, and identify attack traffic
- Identify potentially malicious activity and brute force attempts in Apache Web logs to determine if an attack was successful on a given target
- Dissect the header information in an HTTP request to determine whether a particular request is undesirable or a normal and expected HTTP session
- Analyze Web traffic using a Web analytics tool (Webalizer) to identify website visitors and other statistics gathered from a Web log file
- Use Internet-based tools and research commercial Web analysis tools to identify which is the most appropriate for different business needs

TOOLS AND SOFTWARE	
NAME	**MORE INFORMATION**
Damn Vulnerable Web Application (DVWA)	http://www.dvwa.co.uk/
PuTTY	http://www.chiark.greenend.org.uk/~sgtatham/putty/
tcpdump	http://www.tcpdump.org/

Deliverables

Upon completion of this lab, you are required to provide the following deliverables to your instructor:

1. lab3headers.txt from the brute force attack;
2. Tcpdump log file from TargetUbuntu01;
3. Lab Assessment Questions & Answers for Lab #3.

Hands-On Steps

1. This lab begins at the student landing vWorkstation virtual machine desktop of the VSCL, as shown here.

"Student Landing" VSCL workstation

> **Note:**
> The next steps will use SSH to connect to the lab's Web server, TargetUbuntu01, to configure tcpdump to capture Web traffic on that server.

2. **Double-click** the **PuTTY icon** on the desktop to open the PuTTY application.

   PuTTY is a free utility that can open secure remote connections over the Internet via Telnet or SSH (secure shell).

3. In the PuTTY application window, **type** the IP address for the TargetUbuntu01 server, **172.30.0.4**. **Select** the **SSH radio button** and **click** the **Open button** to start the connection.

Using PuTTY to connect to TargetUbuntu01

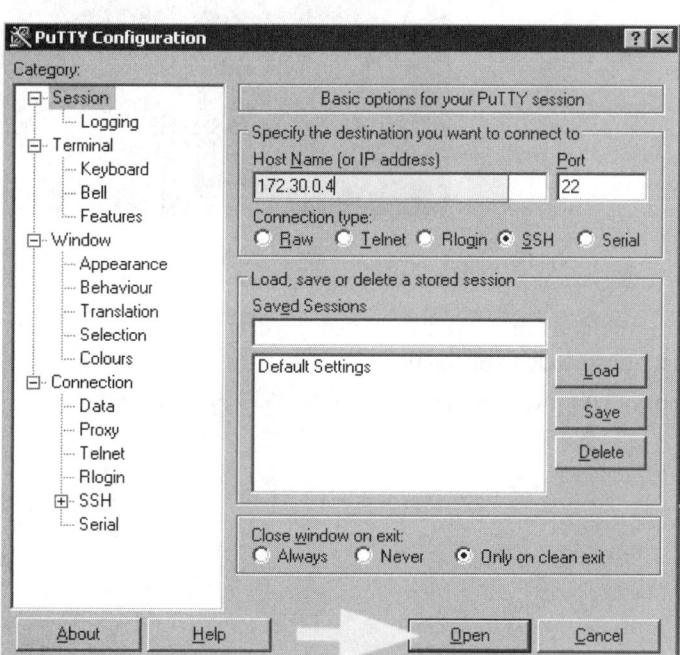

4. PuTTY will launch a terminal console window. At the login prompt, **type** the following credentials:
   - Username: **student**
   - Password: **ISS316Security**

PuTTY terminal console
window

5. At the command prompt, **type ifconfig –a** and **press Enter** to verify the IP address for the server.

   The IP address is displayed after the abbreviation *inet addr* in the eth0 section of the results. eth0 is the interface used to access TargetUbuntu01. This IP address should match the one you entered in the PuTTY application window.

Finding the IP address
for TargetUbuntu01

6. At the command prompt, **type sudo ifconfig eth0 promisc** and **press Enter** to set the eth0 interface card to promiscuous mode to allow packet capturing.

7. When prompted for a sudo password, **type ISS316Security**.

8. At the command prompt, **type sudo tcpdump –i eth0 –w /home/student/lab3.txt tcp port 80** and **press Enter** to configure tcpdump to monitor Web traffic and write the results to a file that can be analyzed later.

Configuring tcpdump

```
student@targetubuntu: ~                                          _ □ ×
              inet addr:172.30.0.4  Bcast:172.30.0.255  Mask:255.255.255.0
              inet6 addr: fe80::2c6b:bdff:fe4b:fb10/64 Scope:Link
              UP BROADCAST RUNNING MULTICAST  MTU:1500  Metric:1
              RX packets:364 errors:0 dropped:0 overruns:0 frame:0
              TX packets:78 errors:0 dropped:0 overruns:0 carrier:0
              collisions:0 txqueuelen:1000
              RX bytes:30403 (30.4 KB)  TX bytes:13457 (13.4 KB)
              Interrupt:32 Base address:0x8000

lo            Link encap:Local Loopback
              inet addr:127.0.0.1  Mask:255.0.0.0
              inet6 addr: ::1/128 Scope:Host
              UP LOOPBACK RUNNING  MTU:16436  Metric:1
              RX packets:4 errors:0 dropped:0 overruns:0 frame:0
              TX packets:4 errors:0 dropped:0 overruns:0 carrier:0
              collisions:0 txqueuelen:0
              RX bytes:240 (240.0 B)  TX bytes:240 (240.0 B)

student@targetubuntu:~$ sudo ifconfig eth0 promisc
[sudo] password for student:
student@targetubuntu:~$ sudo tcpdump –i eth0 -w /home/student/lab3.txt tcp port
80
tcpdump: listening on eth0, link-type EN10MB (Ethernet), capture size 96 bytes
```

9. **Minimize** the **PuTTY terminal window**.

> **Note:**
> The next steps will use the Firefox browser to access the Damn Vulnerable Web Application (DVWA) to perform a brute force attack on the Web server and capture data using the Live HTTP Headers plug-in.

10. **Double-click** the **Mozilla Firefox icon** on the desktop to open the Firefox browser.

    You can access the DVWA tool using any Internet browser, but the steps in this lab will use the Firefox browser.

11. In the Firefox browser's toolbar, **click Tools** and then **click Live HTTP headers** in the menu to turn on this option.

    The Live HTTP headers add-on allows the user to view the HTTP header of any page viewed in the Firefox browser.

Live HTTP headers option on the Firefox browser

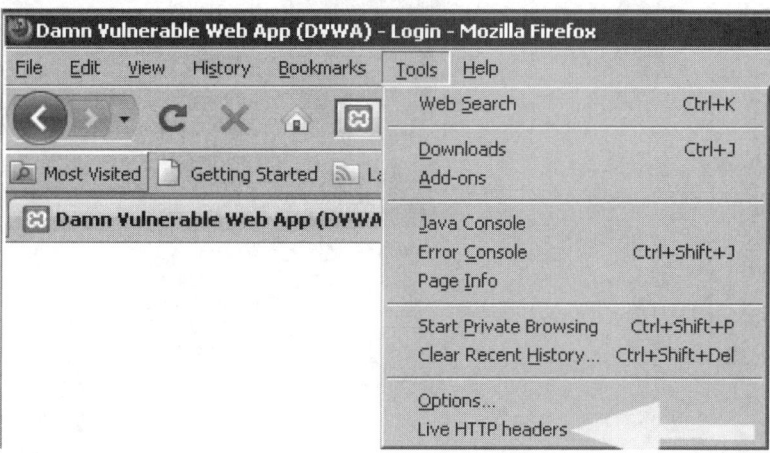

3

Perform a Post-Mortem Review of a Data Breach Incident

12. **Minimize** the **Live HTTP headers dialog box**.

13. In the browser's address box, **type http://172.30.0.4/dvwa** and **press Enter** to open the Damn Vulnerable Web Application.

   DVWA is a Web application that is made purposefully vulnerable. It is installed on a local Web server to allow security analysts a safe place to test the security of their applications.

14. **Log in** to the application with the following credentials and **click Login** to continue:
   - Username: **admin**
   - Password: **password**

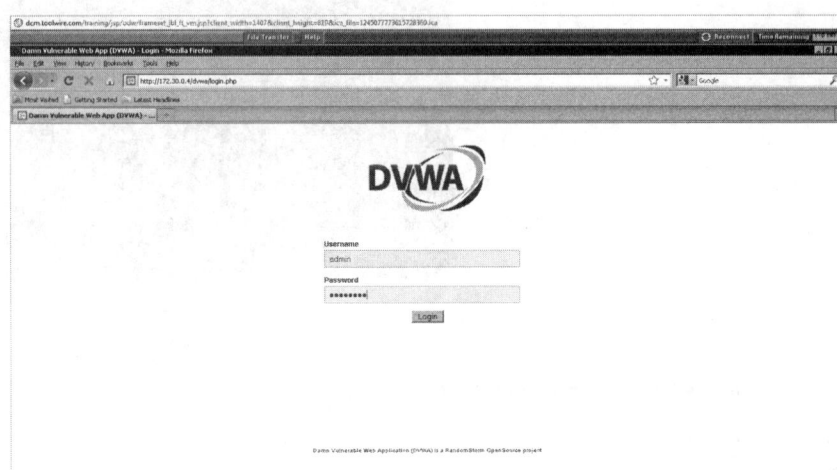

15. On the DVWA Welcome screen, **click** the **DVWA Security button**.

16. **Select low** from the Script Security drop-down menu and **click Submit** to change the security level.

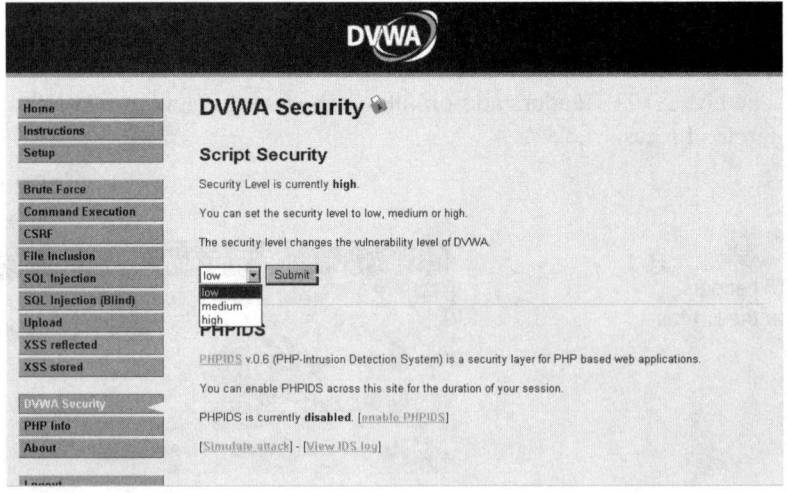

17. **Click** the **Brute Force button** in the DVWA navigation menu.

The brute force attack is a trial and error method for detecting username/password combinations.

18. On the Vulnerability: Brute Force page, **attempt a brute force login** in DVWA using the following credentials and then **press Login**:

- Username: **test**
- Password: **lab3**

FIGURE 3.9

Attempting a brute force login attack

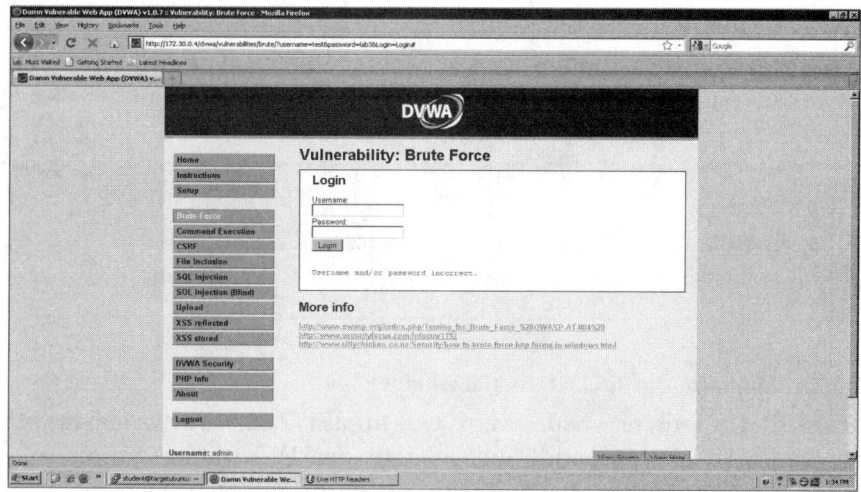

The DVWA tool will return an invalid username/password error.

19. **Maximize** the **Live HTTP headers dialog box**.

The dialog box will display the HTML code for the header of the active Web page, in this case, the DVWA application.

FIGURE 3.10

Live HTTP headers dialog box

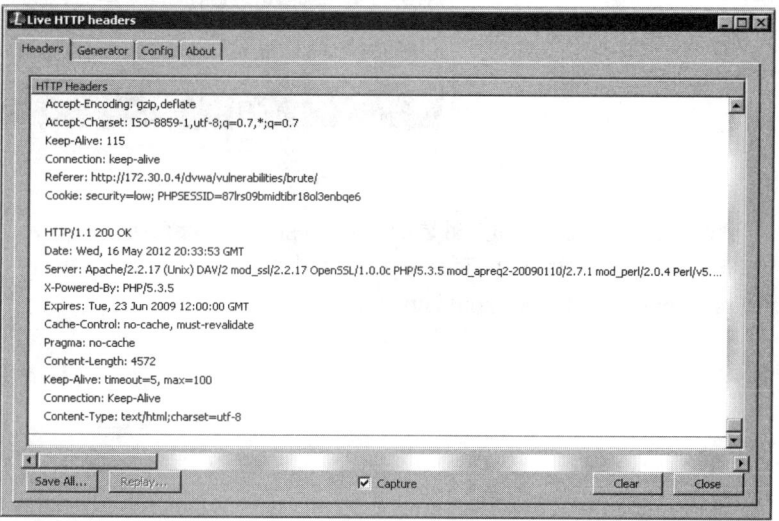

20. **Click** the **Save All button** in the Live HTTP headers dialog box and save the file as **lab3headers.txt** to the vWorkstation desktop.

21. Use the **File Transfer button** to **download** the **lab3headers.txt file** and **submit** it to your instructor as part of your deliverables for this lab.

22. **Close** the **Live HTTP headers dialog box**.

23. **Maximize** the **PuTTY terminal window**.

24. From the terminal window, **hold CTRL** and **press Z** to stop the tcpdump capture process.

25. At the command prompt, **type sudo tcpdump –r /home/student/lab3.txt** and **press Enter** to view the results of the tcpdump onscreen. You will use this information to complete the deliverables for this lab.

26. **Make a screen capture** of the tcpdump results and **paste** it into a new text document. You may have to take multiple screen captures to display the entire output.

> ▶ **Note:**
> To capture the screen, **press** the **Ctrl** and **PrtSc** keys together, and then **use Ctrl + V** to paste the image into a Word or other word processor document.

27. **Minimize** the **PuTTY terminal window**.

28. In the browser's address box, **type http://172.30.0.4/dvwa/nopage.html** to open a non-existent page in the DVWA application and generate some Web traffic.

    The browser will display a 404 error indicating that the page cannot be found.

29. **Maximize** the **PuTTY terminal window**.

30. At the command prompt, **type sudo webalizer** and **press Enter** to process the most recent Web traffic logs with the Webalizer tool.

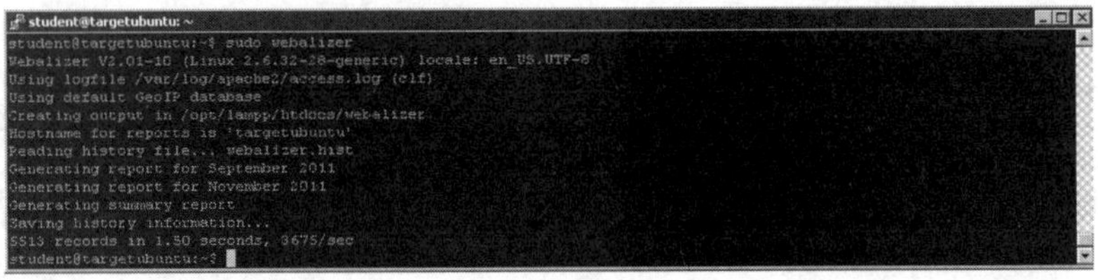

FIGURE 3.11

Generating the
Webalizer report

31. **Make a screen capture** of the Webalizer results and **paste** it into your text document. You may have to take multiple screen captures to display the entire output.

32. **Minimize** the **PuTTY terminal window**.

33. In the browser's address box, **type http://172.30.0.4/webalizer** to view statistics from the Web logs.

FIGURE 3.12

Viewing usage statistics
for TargetUbuntu01

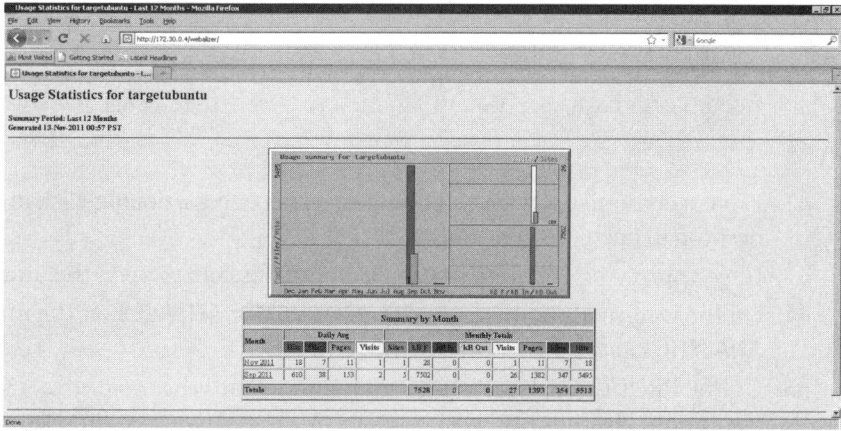

34. **Make a screen capture** of the Webalizer results and **paste** it into your text document. You may have to take multiple screen captures to display the entire output.

35. **Review** the type of statistics available from the Webalizer tool.

36. **Maximize** the **PuTTY terminal window**.

37. At the command prompt, **type sudo grep lab /var/log/apache2/access.log** and **press Enter** to view the raw Web log file.

The system will return the details of the brute force attack from step 18 above.

FIGURE 3.13

Using the grep
command to review Web
server log files

38. **Make a screen capture** of the log file results and **paste** it into your text document.

39. **Close** the **PuTTY terminal window. Click** the **OK button** if prompted to confirm your choice to exit the PuTTY session.

40. **Close** the **Mozilla Firefox window**.

41. Use the **File Transfer button** to **download** your **text document** and **submit** it to your instructor as part of your deliverables for this lab.

 Note:

The next steps will use a computer with Internet access to research the capabilities of some popular Web analytics tools. You will need this information to complete the deliverables for this lab.

42. From a computer workstation with Internet access, **double-click** any **Internet browser icon** on your desktop to open the application.

43. In your browser's address box, **type webtrends.com** to open the analytics tool.

44. On the webtrends homepage, **click PRODUCTS + SERVICES** on the main navigation menu and **click ANALYTICS** in the drop-down menu.

45. On the PRODUCTS + SERVICES submenu toward the top of the ANALYTICS page, **click each link** (Overview, Heatmaps, Website, Social, Mobile, Advanced, and Integrations) to discover the capabilities of this tool.

46. In your browser's address box, **type google.com/analytics** to open the analytics tool.

47. On the Google Analytics page, **click Features** from the main navigation bar.

48. **Click each link** (Analysis Tools, Content, Mobile, Conversion, Social, and Advertising) on the Features submenu to discover the capabilities of this tool.

49. In your browser's address box, **type web.analytics.yahoo.com** to open the analytics tool.

50. On the Yahoo! Web Analytics page, **click Features** from the main navigation bar to discover the capabilities of this tool.

51. **Close** the **browser window**.

Evaluation Criteria and Rubrics

The following are the evaluation criteria and rubrics for Lab #3 that students must perform:

1. Was the student able to analyze Web traffic in real time using tcpdump to capture traffic as it happens on the network and identify attack traffic? – [**20%**]

2. Was the student able to identify potentially malicious activity and brute force attempts in Apache Web logs to determine if an attack was successful on a given target? – [**20%**]

3. Was the student able to dissect the header information in an HTTP request to determine whether a particular request is undesirable or a normal and expected HTTP session? – [**20%**]

4. Was the student able to analyze Web traffic using a Web analytics tool (Webalizer) to identify website visitors and other statistics gathered from a Web log file? – [**20%**]

5. Was the student able to use Internet-based tools and research commercial Web analysis tools to identify which is the most appropriate for different business needs? – [**20%**]

LAB #3 – ASSESSMENT WORKSHEET

Perform a Post-Mortem Review of a Data Breach Incident

Course Name and Number:

_____

Student Name:

_____

Instructor Name:

_____

Lab Due Date:

_____

Overview

In this lab, you performed a live brute force attack on the TargetUbuntu01 Web server and configured tcpdump to capture traffic on the Web server while the brute force attack was occurring. You also dissected HTTP header information to determine desirable and undesirable session types and used Webalizer, a Web analysis tool, to investigate statistics gathered from Web logs. Finally, you explored how Google analytics and Yahoo! analytics can be used for search-engine optimization.

Lab Assessment Questions & Answers

1. What is the purpose and function of Google analytics?

_____

_____

_____

_____

_____

2. What is the purpose of performing ongoing website traffic analysis and Web trending analysis on production Web servers and websites?

_____

_____

_____

_____

3. How can tcpdump be used as a critical Web server tool for conducting ongoing traffic monitoring and traffic analysis?

_____

_____

_____

_____

_____

4. How can the various modes of verbose in tcpdump provide more information for analysis?

_____

_____

_____

_____

_____

5. Using the saved file from the Live HTTP Headers tool, what is the user-agent used by the client browser?

_____

_____

_____

_____

6. Using the saved file from the Live HTTP Headers tool, what information can you gather just from the HTTP headers?

_____

_____

_____

_____

_____

_____

_____

3

Perform a Post-Mortem Review of a Data Breach Incident

7. How could tcpdump be used to capture passwords sent to a website?

8. Why is it more appropriate to submit sensitive information using HTTP POST than HTTP GET?

9. How can Webalizer aid in the interpretation of Web log files?

10. How do tools such as Google Analytics work to track website traffic?

Exploit Known Web Vulnerabilities on a Live Web Server

Introduction

In this lab, you will evaluate a list of the 10 most critical Web application security risks as determined by the Open Web Application Security Project (OWASP). You also will use the Damn Vulnerable Web Application (DVWA) to perform some of the most common Web application attacks: a brute force attack, a cross-site request forgery (CSRF) attack, a file inclusion (upload) attack, an SQL injection attack, and a cross-site scripting attack (XSS). Finally, you will describe how hackers might use these types of attacks to compromise websites and Web applications.

Learning Objectives

Upon completing this lab, you will be able to:

- Evaluate the most common Web vulnerabilities using the OWASP Top 10 and make recommendations based on best practices
- Execute an HTML form brute force attack, and exploit a Web application by issuing arbitrary commands through an HTML input form
- Exploit a Web application using cross-site request forgery (CSRF) and cross-site scripting (XSS) victimizing logged-in users to a Web application to gain an understanding of how attackers exploit vulnerability and what countermeasures can be implemented
- Compromise an SQL database for confidential data using an SQL injection and extract PII from a vulnerable backend
- Obtain administrator access on a Web application using file path injection and CSRF to understand the risks associated with allowing file uploads and dynamic file inclusion

TOOLS AND SOFTWARE	
NAME	**MORE INFORMATION**
Damn Vulnerable Web Application (DVWA)	http://www.dvwa.co.uk/

Deliverables

Upon completion of this lab, you are required to provide the following deliverables to your instructor:

1. Web Application Security Risk Assessment;
2. Lab Assessment Questions & Answers for Lab #4.

Hands-On Steps

1. This lab begins at the student landing vWorkstation virtual machine desktop of the VSCL, as shown here.

"Student Landing" VSCL workstation

2. **Review** the **OWASP Top 10 - 2010** handout for this lab. The document from the Open Web Application Security Project lists the top 10 most critical Web application security risks.

   If not available from your instructor, **use** the **File Transfer button** on the vWorkstation virtual machine to download this file from the Security_Strategies folder (**C:Security_StrategiesWebSecurityOWAS_ Top_10_-_2010.pdf**).

3. In a new text document, **create** a **Web Application Security Risk Assessment** and **describe** how hackers might use the types of attacks you will practice in this lab, and those detailed in the handout you read in step 2 above, to compromise websites and Web applications.

   You will be responsible for determining what to document in this assessment based on the actions you perform in this lab. After each test, update your text document.

> **Note:**
> The next steps will use the Firefox browser to access the Damn Vulnerable Web Application (DVWA) and set the application's script security level to low which will expose its vulnerabilities for testing.

4. **Double-click** the **Mozilla Firefox icon** on the desktop to open the Firefox browser.

   You can access the DVWA tool using any Internet browser, but the steps in this lab will use the Firefox browser.

5. In the browser's address box, **type http://172.30.0.4/dvwa** and **press Enter** to open the Damn Vulnerable Web Application.

   DVWA is a Web application that is made purposefully vulnerable. It is installed on a local Web server to allow security analysts a safe place to test the security of their applications.

6. **Log in** to the application with the following credentials and **click Login** to continue:
   - Username: **admin**
   - Password: **password**

FIGURE 4.2

DVWA login screen

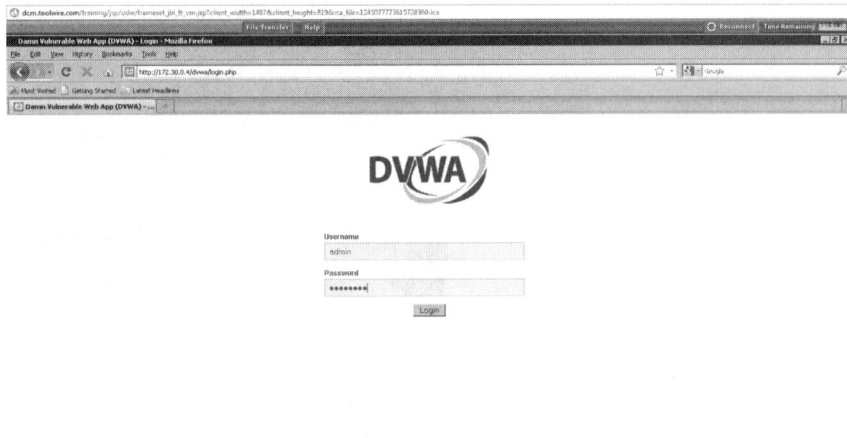

7. On the DVWA Welcome screen, **click** the **DVWA Security button**.
8. **Select low** from the Script Security drop-down menu and **click Submit** to change the security level.

FIGURE 4.3

Changing the script
security level in DVWA

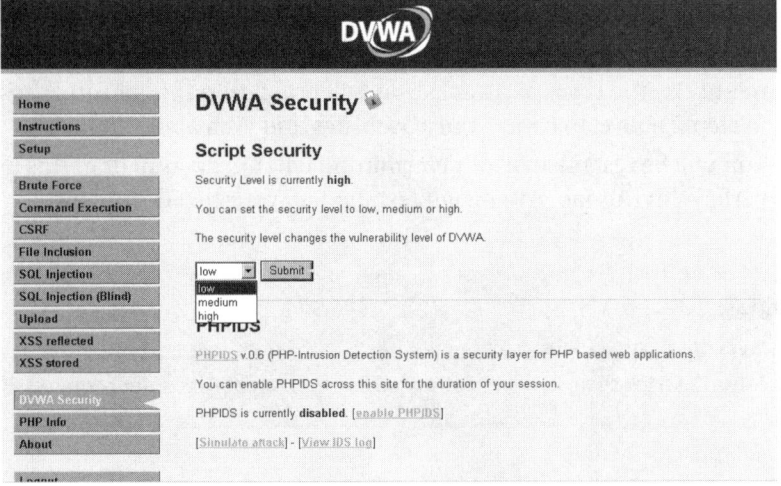

> **Note:**
> The next steps will use the Damn Vulnerable Web Application (DVWA) to perform a brute force attack on the Web server, exploit a Web application using CSRF and XSS, compromise an SQL database using SQL injection, and obtain administrator access to a Web application using file path injection.

9. **Click** the **Brute Force button** in the DVWA navigation menu.

   The brute force attack is a trial and error method for detecting username/password combinations. The vWorkstation machine does not have access to the Internet, but you can type the URLs that appear in the More info section of the page into the browser of a computer with Internet access to learn more about this type of vulnerability.

10. On the Vulnerability: Brute Force page, **attempt a brute force login** in DVWA using the following credentials and then **press Login**:

    * Username: **test**
    * Password: **lab4**

FIGURE 4.4

Attempting a brute force login attack

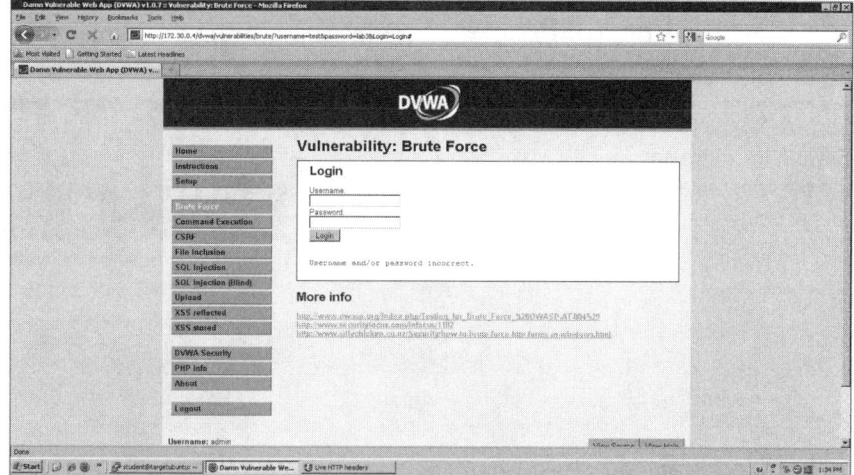

The DVWA tool will return an invalid username/password error.

11. **Click** the **Command Execution button** in the DVWA navigation menu.

    The command execution test allows you to execute OS commands, such as ping, via the Web server. The vWorkstation machine does not have access to the Internet, but you can type the URLs that appear in the More info section of the page into the browser of a computer with Internet access to learn more about this type of vulnerability.

12. On the Ping for FREE section of the page, **type 172.30.0.2** and **click Submit** to ping the vWorkstation.

    The replies returned by the DVWA tool indicate that the virtual machine is accepting requests.

13. In the same box, **type 172.30.0.2; cat /etc/passwd** and **click Submit** to output the contents of the user file on the Linux workstation that is hosting the DVWA tool.

FIGURE 4.5

Exploiting a command execution vulnerability on DVWA

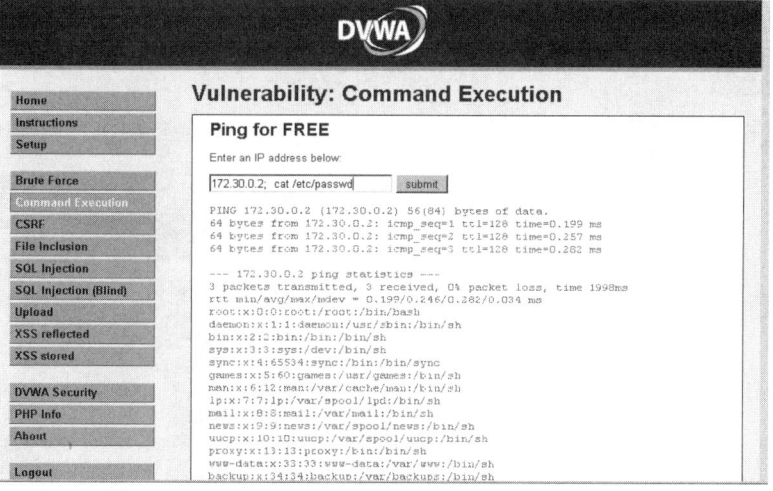

4

Exploit Known Web Vulnerabilities on a Live Web Server

14. **Click** the **CSRF button** in the DVWA navigation menu.

    The cross-site request forgery test allows you to trick a valid user into passing malicious code. The vWorkstation machine does not have access to the Internet, but you can type the URLs that appear in the More info section of the page into the browser of a computer with Internet access to learn more about this type of vulnerability.

15. As a valid user of the Web application, **type** the following data into the relevant boxes on the CSRF page and **click Change** to change the admin password:

    • New password: **test**
    • Confirm new password: **test**

    The CSRF indicates a successful password change in text below the Change button and in the code embedded into the URL (http://172.30.0.4/dvwa/vulnerabilities/csrf/?password_new=test&password_conf=test&Change=Change#). It is that query string that forces the password change.

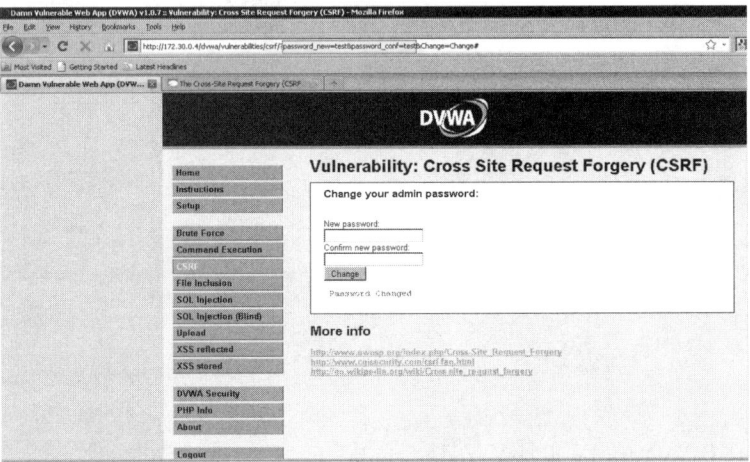

FIGURE 4.6

Viewing the username and password in a URL query string

16. **Click** the **File Inclusion button** in the DVWA navigation menu.

    The file inclusion test allows you to include a remote file by altering the script embedded into the URL. The vWorkstation machine does not have access to the Internet, but you can type the URLs that appear in the More info section of the page into the browser of a computer with Internet access to learn more about this type of vulnerability.

17. **Review** the **URL** on this page: *?page=index.php* is a file inclusion script.

18. **Highlight index.php** in the URL and **type** **../../../../../../etc/passwd**, so that the complete URL reads: **http://172.30.0.4/dvwa/vulnerabilities/fi/?page=../../../../../../etc/passwd**, and **press Enter** to submit the script.

    The DVWA displays the contents of the server user account file on the screen.

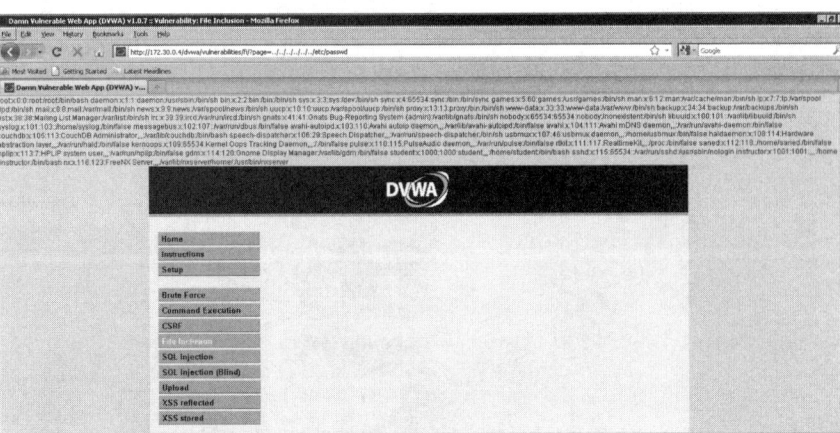

FIGURE 4.7

Exploiting file inclusion vulnerability on DVWA

19. **Click** the **SQL Injection button** in the DVWA navigation menu.

    The SQL injection test allows you to include malicious scripts in a Web form. The vWorkstation machine does not have access to the Internet, but you can type the URLs that appear in the More info section of the page into the browser of a computer with Internet access to learn more about this type of vulnerability.

20. In the User ID box, **type a' OR '1'='1'#,** and **click Submit.**

    The DVWA tool will return the first and last names of everyone in the application's database.

21. **Click** the **Upload button** in the DVWA navigation menu.

    The file upload test allows you to send a malicious file to the Web server. The vWorkstation machine does not have access to the Internet, but you can type the URLs that appear in the More info section of the page into the browser of a computer with Internet access to learn more about this type of vulnerability.

22. **Minimize** the **Mozilla Firefox window**.

23. From the vWorkstation desktop, **click** the **Windows Start button** and **click Run.**

24. In the Run dialog box, **type notepad** and **click** the **OK button** to create a new file that you will upload in a later step.

25. In the Notepad window, **type** the following HTML code:

    <html>

    <title>TEST</title>

    <body>

    <img src="http://172.30.0.4/dvwa/vulnerabilities/csrf/?password_new=changedit&password_conf=changedit&Change=Change#" width="1" height="1" boarder="0">

    Test Page. Please Ignore.

    </body>

    </html>

    The HTML code includes the CSRF query string that will change the admin password to *changedit*.

26. In the Notepad menu, **click File > Save As** to open the Save As dialog box.

27. **Click** the **Desktop icon**, **select All Files** from the Save as type drop-down menu, **type change.php** in the File name box, and **click Save.**

Saving a php file in Notepad

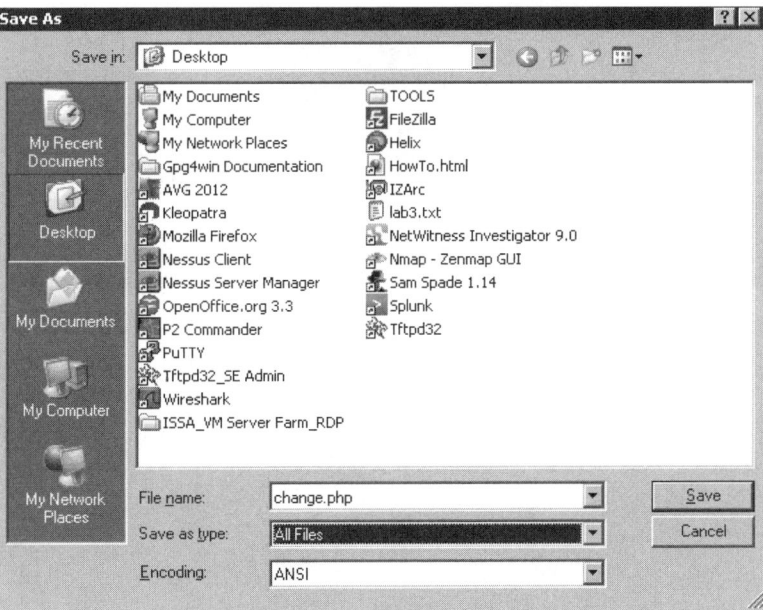

28. **Close** the **Notepad**.
29. **Maximize** the **Mozilla Firefox browser**.
30. On the Upload page, **click** the **Browse button** to open the File Upload dialog box.
31. **Click** the **Desktop icon**, **click** the **change.php file** in the resulting list, and **click** the **Open button** to add the file to the Choose an image to upload box.
32. **Click** the **Upload button** to send the file to the Web server.

    The DVWA tool returns a message indicating that the file was successfully uploaded and displays the query string used by the server to upload the file: *../../hackable/uploads/change.php.*

33. **Click** the **File Inclusion button** in the DVWA navigation menu to return to that test page.
34. **Review** the **URL** on this page: *?page=index.php* is a file inclusion script.
35. **Highlight index.php** in the URL and **type ../../hackable/uploads/change.php**, so that the complete URL reads: **http://172.30.0.4/dvwa/vulnerabilities/fi/?page=../../hackable/uploads/change.php**, and **press Enter** to submit the script.

    The DVWA displays a message that reads: *Test Page. Please Ignore.* (This is the text included in the change.php file you created in step 25 above.) The message indicates that the file inclusion was successful and the admin password has changed to *changedit*.

36. **Click** the **Logout button** at the bottom of the DVWA navigation menu to return to the DVWA login screen to verify that the exploit worked.
37. **Log in** to the application with the following credentials and **click Login** to continue:
    * Username: **admin**
    * Password: **changedit**

    A successful login indicates that the exploit embedded in the change.php file worked. If you are not able to log in using the *changedit* password, try again using the original password, *password,* or use the following alternate credentials and repeat steps 22-37 to attempt the change again:
    * Username: **pablo**
    * Password: **letmein**

38. **Click** the **XSS reflected button** in the DVWA navigation menu.

    The reflected cross-site scripting test allows you to add client-side script into a Web page viewed by other users. The vWorkstation machine does not have access to the Internet, but you can type the URLs that appear in the More info section of the page into the browser of a computer with Internet access to learn more about this type of vulnerability.

39. In the What's your name? box, **type Simon** and **click Submit**.

The intent of the Web form is to take the name you entered and repeat it back to you as a friendly welcome.

FIGURE 4.9

Expected output from
XSS test

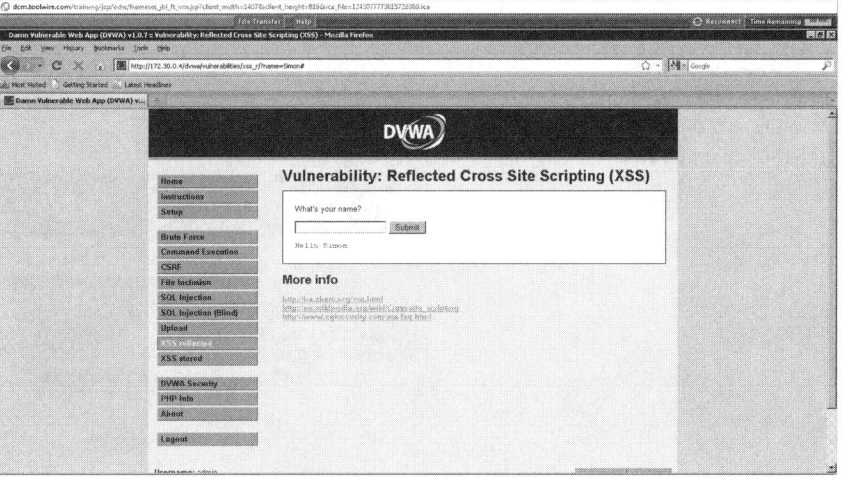

40. In the What's your name? box, **type <script>alert('GOTCHA');</script>** and **click Submit**.

The Web form processes the script and returns a pop-up alert window, which indicates that any script could be processed by this Web form.

FIGURE 4.10

Exploiting an XSS
vulnerability on DVWA

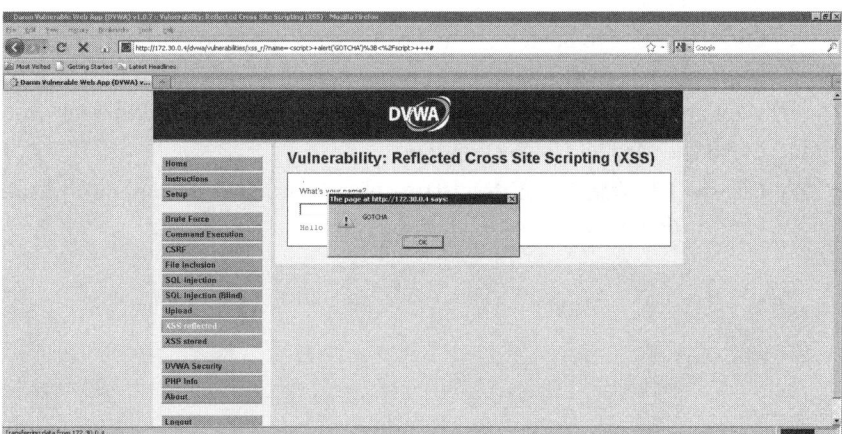

41. **Click** the **OK button** to close the alert window.

42. **Click** the **XSS stored button** in the DVWA navigation menu.

The stored cross-site scripting test allows you to collect data that is stored on a Web server visited by a valid user. The vWorkstation machine does not have access to the Internet, but you can type the URLs that appear in the More info section of the page into the browser of a computer with Internet access to learn more about this type of vulnerability.

43. In the relevant boxes, **type** the following information and **click Sign Guestbook**:
    * Name*: **Student**
    * Message*: **I love studying.<script>alert('GOTCHA');</script>**

    The DVWA tool displays the pop-up alert message.

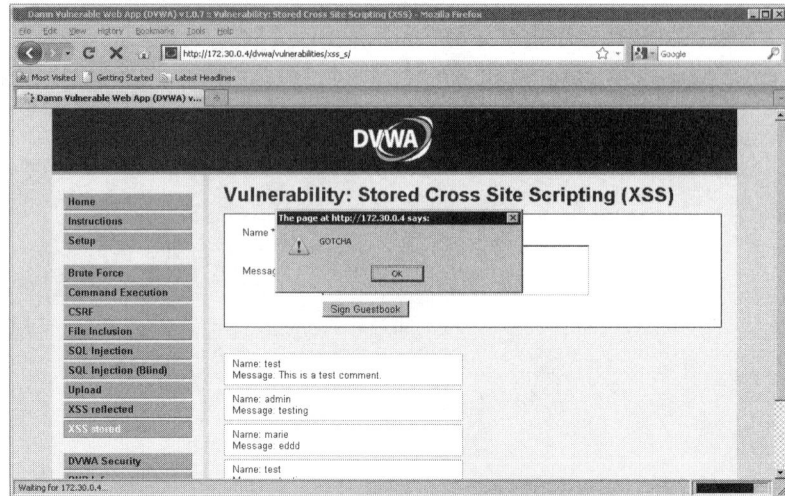

44. **Click** the **OK button** to close the alert window.

    The DVWA tool has posted your message with no visible indication that there is script embedded on the page.

45. **Click** the **Refresh button** in the browser's toolbar to reload the page.

    The DVWA tool displays the pop-up alert message again indicating that the script now resides in the Web application database and will work each time a valid user enters the page.

46. **Close** the **Mozilla Firefox window.**

47. Use the **File Transfer button** to **download** your **text document** and **submit** it to your instructor as part of your deliverables for this lab.

Evaluation Criteria and Rubrics

The following are the evaluation criteria and rubrics for Lab #4 that students must perform:

1. Was the student able to evaluate the most common Web vulnerabilities using the OWASP Top 10 and make recommendations based on best practices? – **[20%]**

2. Was the student able to execute an HTML form brute force attack and exploit a Web application by issuing arbitrary commands through an HTML input form? – **[20%]**

3. Was the student able to exploit a Web application using cross-site request forgery (CSRF) and cross-site scripting (XSS) victimizing logged-in users to a Web application to gain an understanding of how attackers exploit vulnerability and what countermeasures can be implemented? – **[20%]**

4. Was the student able to compromise an SQL database for confidential data using an SQL injection and extract PII from a vulnerable backend? – **[20%]**

5. Was the student able to obtain administrator access on a Web application using file path injection and CSRF to understand the risks associated with allowing file uploads and dynamic file inclusion? – **[20%]**

Exploit Known Web Vulnerabilities on a Live Web Server

Course Name and Number:

_____

Student Name:

_____

Instructor Name:

_____

Lab Due Date:

_____

Overview

In this lab, you evaluated a list of the 10 most critical Web application security risks as determined by the Open Web Application Security Project (OWASP). You also used the Damn Vulnerable Web Application (DVWA) to perform some of the most common Web application attacks: a brute force attack, a cross-site request forgery (CSRF) attack, a file inclusion (upload) attack, an SQL injection attack, and a cross-site scripting attack (XSS). Finally, you described how hackers might use these types of attacks to compromise websites and Web applications.

Lab Assessment Questions & Answers

1. What is a brute force attack and how can the risks of these attacks be mitigated?

_____

_____

_____

_____

_____

_____

2. Explain a scenario where a hacker may use cross-site request forgery (CRFS) to perform authorized transactions.

_____

_____

_____

_____

_____

_____

_____

3. What is the proper way to prevent XSS attacks?

_____

_____

_____

_____

4. If an attacker wishes to place a phishing page on a website, what is a common vulnerability that can be exploited to successfully do this?

_____

_____

_____

_____

_____

5. What could be the impact of a successful SQL injection?

_____

_____

_____

_____

4

Exploit Known Web Vulnerabilities on a Live Web Server

6. What is the difference between a blind SQL injection attack and a normal SQL injection attack?

_____

_____

_____

_____

7. Why are stored XSS vulnerabilities a major risk factor for Web applications?

_____

_____

_____

_____

8. What would the following URL being queued in your Web logs be an indication of? "http://www.testurl. com/../../../../../../../../../../../etc/passwd"

_____

_____

_____

_____

9. How would you ensure security between a Web application and an SQL server?

_____

_____

_____

_____

10. What is a benefit of using a Web application firewall (WAF)?

_____

_____

_____

_____

Apply OWASP to a Web Security Assessment

Introduction

In this lab, you will review the Open Web Application Security Project (OWASP) website and its Web application test methodology. You will review the standards and guides published by this project and compile a research report on your findings. You also will draft a Web Application Test Plan based on the information you gained in your OWASP research.

This lab is a paper-based design lab and does not require use of the Virtual Security Cloud Lab (VSCL). To successfully complete the deliverables for this lab, you will need access to a text editor or word processor, such as Microsoft® Word. For some labs, you may also need access to a graphics line drawing application, such as Visio or PowerPoint.

> **Note:**
> If you don't have a word processor or graphics package, use OpenOffice on the student landing vWorkstation for your lab deliverables and to answer the lab assessment questions. To capture screenshots, **press Prt Sc >
> MSPAINT, paste** into a text document, and **save** the document in the Security_Strategies folder (**C:\Security_
> Strategies**) using the File Transfer function.

Learning Objectives

Upon completing this lab, you will be able to:

- Plan for a Web assessment using the OWASP Application Security Verification Standard Project (ASVS) by reviewing all the available documentation
- Identify secure code review practices and secure testing practices using OWASP tools, and recognize common secure coding principles
- Implement a secure software development framework using the Open Software Assurance Maturity Model (OpenSAMM)
- Identify the key points for a successful code review as outlined by OWASP for maintaining secure coding practices throughout the Web applications on the network
- Create a secure software testing plan as outlined by OWASP

TOOLS AND SOFTWARE	
NAME	**MORE INFORMATION**
None	

Deliverables

Upon completion of this lab, you are required to provide the following deliverables to your instructor:

1. OWASP Research Report;
2. Web Application Test Plan;
3. Lab Assessment Questions & Answers for Lab #5.

Hands-On Steps

1. This lab begins at a workstation with Internet access. **Double-click** any **Internet browser icon** on your desktop to open the application.

> ▶ **Note:**
> The next steps will explore the website and Web application standards recommended by OWASP. You will summarize your research in an OWASP Research Report and a Web Application Test Plan.

2. In a new text document, **create** an **OWASP Research Report**.

   You will be responsible for determining what to document in this report based on your **summary of each of the documents** you will review as part of this lab.

3. In your browser's address box, **type owasp.org** to open the Open Web Application Security Project website

FIGURE 5.1

Viewing the OWASP website

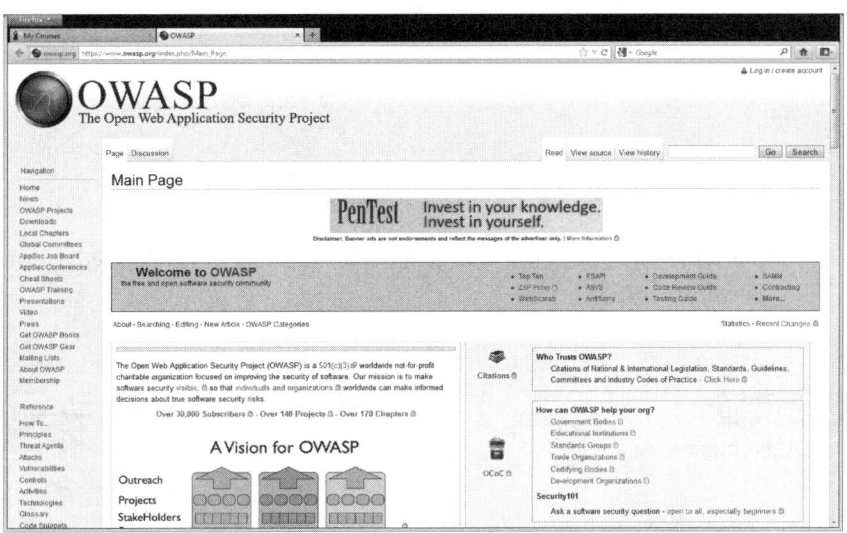

4. In the Welcome to OWASP section of the page, **click SAMM** (Software Assurance Maturity Model).

5. **Click** the **Download SAMM Now icon** on the OpenSAMM page to open the download page.

6. **Click** the download **PDF link**, in your preferred language, and save the OpenSAMM framework to your workstation.

   This document, in English, is also available on the vWorkstation. **Use** the **File Transfer button** to download this file from the Security_Strategies folder (**C:Security_Strategies\WebSecurity\SAMM-1.0.pdf**).

FIGURE 5.2

Downloading the SAMM framework

7. **Read** the document and **review the SAMM framework**. You will need this information to complete the deliverables in this lab.

FIGURE 5.3

The SAMM framework

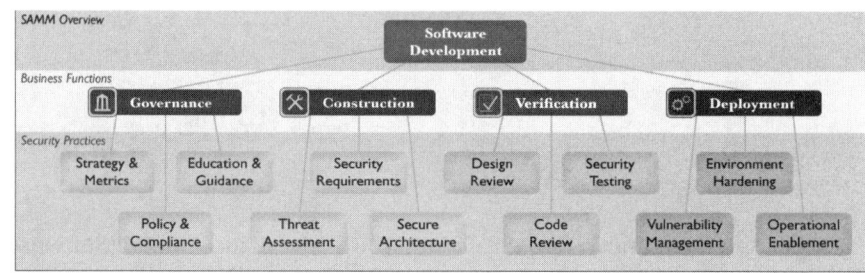

8. From the SAMM download page, **click** the browser's **Back button** to return to the SAMM overview page.

9. **Click OWASP Projects** in the left navigation menu.

10. Use the browser's scrollbar to scroll down to the Subcategories section of the page and **click** the **OWASP Application Security Verification Standard Project link**.

11. **Click** the **Downloads tab** on the Application Security Verification Standard page.

12. **Click** the download **PDF link**, in your preferred language, from the Get ASVS column and **save** the latest version (2009) of this standard to your workstation.

    This document, in English, is also available on the vWorkstation. **Use** the **File Transfer button** to download this file from the Security_Strategies folder (**C:Security_Strategies\WebSecurity\OWASP_ASVS_2009_Web_App_Std_Release.pdf**).

The Application Security
Verification Standard

13. **Review** the Application Security Verification Standard (ASVS) **overview**. You will need this information to complete the deliverables in this lab.

14. From the ASVS Downloads page, **click** the **Project Presentation link**, in your preferred language, from the About ASVS column and **save** the PowerPoint file to your workstation.

The Application Security
Verification Standard

15. **Review** the **presentation**. You will need this information to complete the deliverables in this lab.

16. **Click** the **Home tab** to return to the ASVS homepage.

17. **Click** the **OWASP Development Guide link** from the Related Resources section of the page.

18. Scroll to the Downloads section of the page and **click** the **Development Guide 2005 PDF link**, in your preferred language, from the Get the Development Guide section and **save** this document to your workstation.

    This document, in English, is also available on the vWorkstation. **Use** the **File Transfer button** to download this file from the Security_Strategies folder (**C:Security_Strategies\WebSecurity\ OWASPGuide2.0.1.pdf**).

FIGURE 5.6

The OWASP
Development Guide

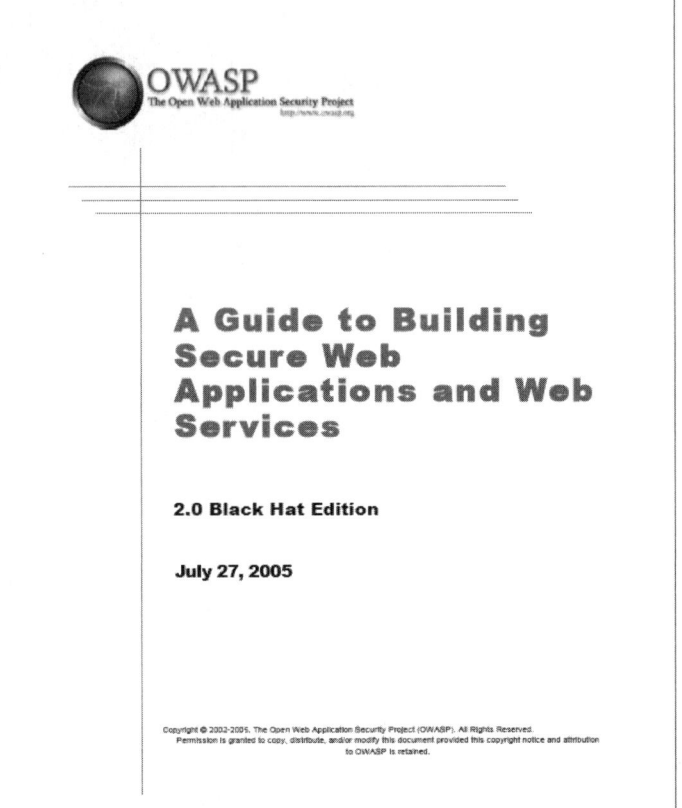

19. **Review** the **Data Validation Strategies** section of the guide. You will need this information to complete the deliverables in this lab.

20. **Click OWASP Projects** in the left navigation menu.

21. Use the browser's scrollbar to scroll down to the Subcategories section of the page and **click** the **OWASP Code Review Project link**.

22. Use the browser's scrollbar to scroll down to the Roadmap section of the page and **click** the **Code Review Guide V1.1 link** from the Last Reviewed Release column.

23. Scroll to the How section of the page, **click** the **OWASP Code Review Guide V1.1 PDF link**, and **save** this document to your workstation.

This document, in English, is also available on the vWorkstation. **Use** the **File Transfer button** to download this file from the Security_Strategies folder (**C:Security_Strategies\WebSecurity\OWASP_ Code_Review_Guide-V1_1.pdf**).

FIGURE 5.7

The OWASP Code
Review Guide

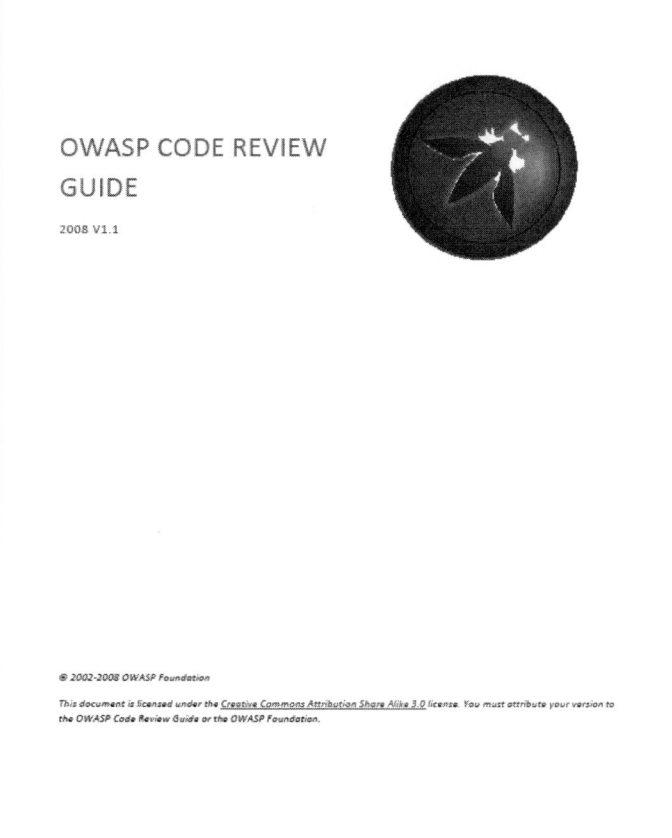

24. **Review** the **Introduction** section of the Code Review Guide. You will need this information to complete the deliverables in this lab.

25. **Click** the browser's **Back button** to return to the OWASP Code Review Project page. Use the browser's scrollbar to scroll down to the Pages in category "OWASP Code Review Project" section of the page and **click** the **Error Handling link**.

26. **Review** the **Error, Exception handling & Logging** section of the page. You will need this information to complete the deliverables in this lab.

27. **Review** the **Generic error messages** section of the page. You will need this information to complete the deliverables in this lab.

28. **Click OWASP Projects** in the left navigation menu.

29. Use the browser's scrollbar to scroll down to the Pages in category "OWASP Project" section of the page and **click** the **OWASP Testing Project link**.

30. Scroll to the Project About section of the page and **click** the **Testing Guide V 3.0 link** in the Last Reviewed Release column.

31. Scroll to the How section of the page and **click** the **OWASP Testing Guide V 3.0 link**, in your preferred language, and **save** this document to your workstation.

    This document is also available on the vWorkstation. **Use** the **File Transfer button** to download this file from the Security_Strategies folder (**C:Security_Strategies\WebSecurity\OWASP_Testing_Guide_v3.pdf**).

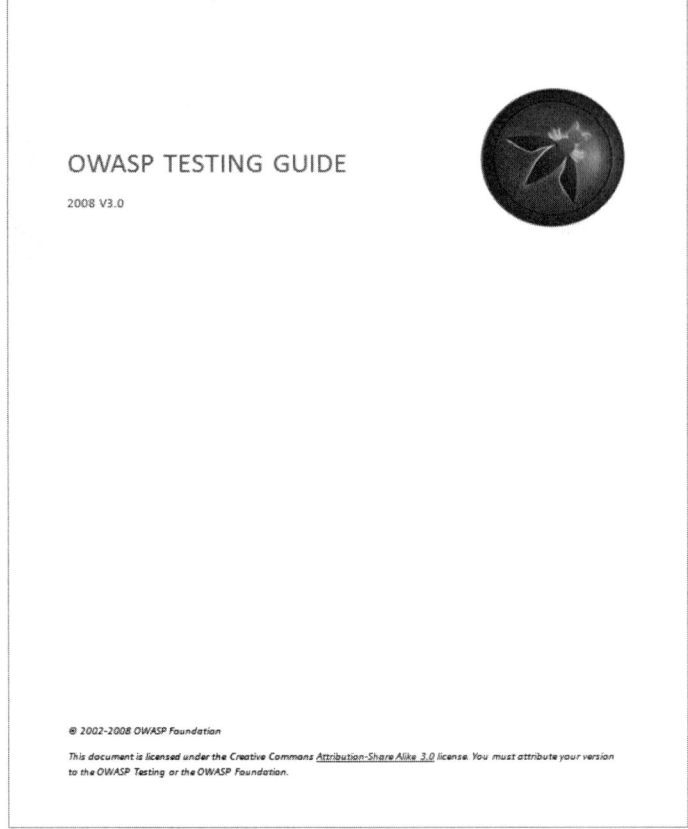

FIGURE 5.8

The OWASP Testing Guide

32. **Review** the **Principles of Testing** section of the document. You will need this information to complete the deliverables in this lab.

33. **Review** the **How to Write the Report of the Testing** section of the document. You will need this information to complete the deliverables in this lab.

34. In a new text document, **create** a **Web Application Test Plan** that includes each of the following elements (you will be responsible for determining what to document in this report based on what you learned in your research):

    - Executive Summary
    - Table of Contents
    - Overview of the tests you would perform and your reasons for including each test

    For this test scenario, assume that you are the network administrator for Online Goodies, an Internet-based company that provides custom promotional gifts, such as T-shirts, mugs, computer accessories, and office décor items, to its corporate customers. This is an e-commerce site that receives most of its income from online credit card purchases. Repeat customers receive discounts based on the amount of their total annual purchases.

35. **Close** the **browser window**.

36. **Submit** both **text documents** to your instructor as deliverables for this lab.

Evaluation Criteria and Rubrics

The following are the evaluation criteria and rubrics for Lab #5 that students must perform:

1. Was the student able to plan for a Web assessment using the OWASP Application Security Verification Standard Project (ASVS) by reviewing all the available documentation? – **[20%]**

2. Was the student able to identify secure code review practices and secure testing practices using OWASP tools, and recognize common secure coding principles? – **[20%]**

3. Was the student able to implement a secure software development framework using the Open Software Assurance Maturity Model (OpenSAMM)? – **[20%]**

4. Was the student able to identify the key points for a successful code review as outlined by OWASP for maintaining secure coding practices throughout the Web applications on the network? – **[20%]**

5. Was the student able to create a secure software testing plan as outlined by OWASP? – **[20%]**

LAB #5 – ASSESSMENT WORKSHEET

Apply OWASP to a Web Security Assessment

Course Name and Number:
_____

Student Name:
_____

Instructor Name:
_____

Lab Due Date:
_____

Overview

In this lab, you reviewed the Open Web Application Security Project (OWASP) website and its Web application test methodology. You reviewed the standards and guides published by this project and compiled a research report on your findings. You also drafted a Web Application Test Plan based on the information you gained in your OWASP research.

Lab Assessment Questions & Answers

1. Identify the four recognized business functions and each security practice of OpenSAMM.

2. Identify and describe the four maturity levels for security practices in SAMM.

_____

_____

_____

_____

_____

3. What are some activities an organization could perform for the security practice of "Threat Assessment"?

_____

_____

_____

_____

4. What are the two recommended assessment styles for SAMM and how are they used?

_____

_____

_____

_____

5. What are the three main objectives of the OWASP Application Security Verification Standard (ASVS) Project?

_____

_____

_____

_____

6. Identify the four levels used for ASVS.

_____

_____

_____

_____

7. According to the OWASP Development Guide, what are some guidelines for handling credit cards on websites?

_____

_____

_____

_____

8. What are the four known data-validation strategies?

_____

_____

_____

_____

9. What are two methods for performing a code review?

_____

_____

_____

_____

10. Why is it important to review how errors are handled during a code review?

_____

_____

_____

_____

11. When should the testing process be introduced in the software development life cycle (SDLC)?

_____

_____

_____

_____

12. What is black-box testing?

_____

_____

_____

_____

13. According to the OWASP Development Guide, what are some basic best practices for handling authentication when designing and developing Web-based software?

_____

_____

_____

_____

14. What is a limitation of automated testing tools?

_____

_____

_____

_____

15. What is meant by the phrase "Test early and test often"?

_____

_____

_____

_____

Align Compliance Requirements to HIPAA, FISMA, GLBA, SOX, PCI DSS, and AICPA

Introduction

In this lab, you will review HIPAA, FISMA, GLBA, SOX, and PCI DSS. You also will discover how to classify an organization for compliance. Finally, you will review the purpose of the AICPA "Trust Services" as they relate to personal privacy.

This lab is a paper-based design lab and does not require use of the Virtual Security Cloud Lab (VSCL). To successfully complete the deliverables for this lab, you will need access to a text editor or word processor, such as Microsoft® Word. For some labs, you may also need access to a graphics line drawing application, such as Visio or PowerPoint.

> **Note:**
>
> If you don't have a word processor or graphics package, use OpenOffice on the student landing vWorkstation for your lab deliverables and to answer the lab assessment questions. To capture screenshots, **press Prt Sc > MSPAINT, paste** into a text document, and **save** the document in the Security_Strategies folder (**C:\Security_Strategies**) using the File Transfer function.

Learning Objectives

Upon completing this lab, you will be able to:

- Identify the criteria for compliance with the Health Insurance Portability and Accountability Act (HIPAA)
- Recognize secure software concepts for federal agencies using the Federal Information Security Management Act (FISMA) Implementation Project
- Identify the security control requirements for the Gramm-Leach-Bliley Act (GLBA) as it pertains to financial institutions
- Determine which organizations must comply with the Sarbanes-Oxley Act (SOX)
- Recognize when a business must comply with the Payment Card Industry Data Security Standard (PCI DSS)
- Review and assess how the American Institute of Certified Public Accountants (AICPA) standardizes the evaluation of consumer privacy during audits with "Trust Services"

TOOLS AND SOFTWARE	
NAME	**MORE INFORMATION**
None	

Deliverables

Upon completion of this lab, you are required to provide the following deliverables to your instructor:

1. Regulatory Compliance Matrix;
2. Organizational Compliance Table;
3. Lab Assessment Questions & Answers for Lab #6.

Hands-On Steps

1. This lab begins at a workstation with Internet access. **Double-click** any **Internet browser icon** on your desktop to open the application.

> **Note:**
> The next steps will explore several regulatory websites. You will use that information to complete the Regulatory Compliance Matrix and the Organizational Compliance Table.

---

2. In your browser's address box, **type http://www.hhs.gov/ocr/privacy/** to open the Department of Health and Human Services' Health Insurance Portability and Accountability Act (HIPAA) website.

FIGURE 6.1

Viewing the HIPAA website

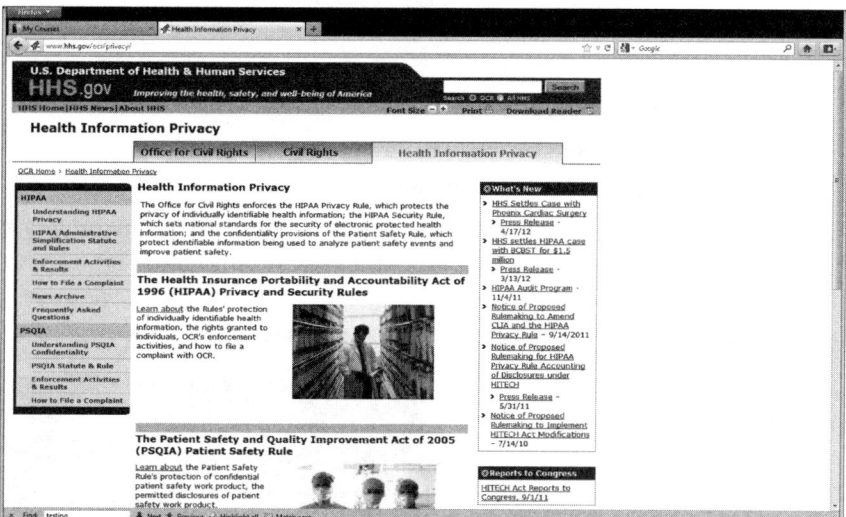

3. **Click** the **Understanding HIPAA Privacy link** in the left navigation menu.
4. **Click** the **For Covered Entities link** in the left navigation menu.
5. **Review** the website to locate the following information:
   - What are the HIPAA compliance requirements?
   - What is protected by the Security Rule?
   - What fines are associated with HIPAA violations?
   - When would a health care provider be required to notify HHS of a security breach?

6. In your browser's address box, **type http://csrc.nist.gov/groups/SMA/fisma/index.html** to open the National Institute of Standards and Technology's Federal Information Security Management Act (FISMA) website.

FIGURE 6.2

Viewing NIST's FISMA website

7. **Click** the **Detailed Overview link** in the left navigation menu.
8. **Review** the website to locate the following information:
   - What are the FISMA compliance requirements?
9. In your browser's address box, **type http://business.ftc.gov/privacy-and-security/gramm-leach-bliley-act** to open the Federal Trade Commission's Gramm-Leach-Bliley Act (GLBA) website.

FIGURE 6.3

Viewing the FTC's GLBA website

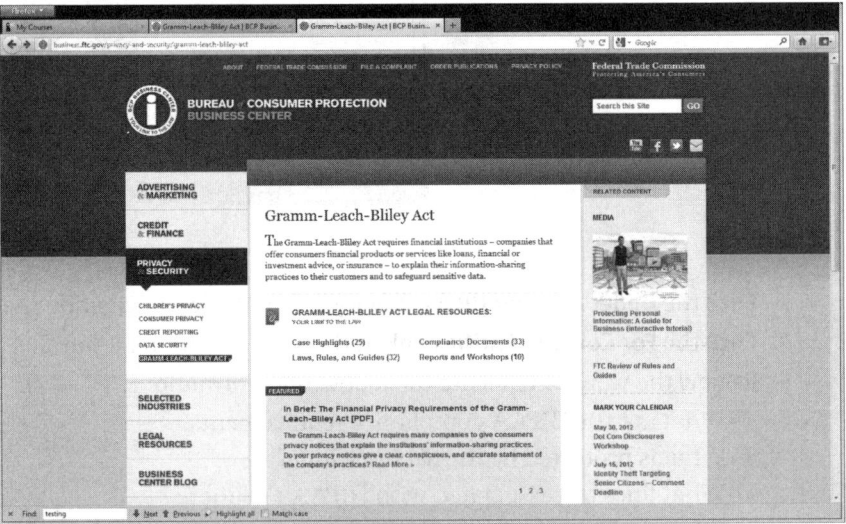

10. **Click** the **In Brief: The Financial Privacy Requirements of the Gramm-Leach-Bliley Act link** in the center of the page.
11. **Review** the website to locate the following information:
    - What are the GLBA compliance requirements?
    - What is the Safeguards Rule?
12. In your browser's address box, **type http://www.sec.gov/spotlight/soxcomp.htm** to open the Securities and Exchange Commission's Sarbanes-Oxley Act (SOX) website.

13. **Click** the **Sarbanes-Oxley Section 404 — A Guide for Small Business link** in the center of the page.

FIGURE 6.4

Viewing the SEC's
SOX website

6

Align Compliance Requirements to HIPAA,
FISMA, GLBA, SOX, PCI DSS, and AICPA

14. **Review** the website to locate the following information:
    - What are the SOX compliance requirements?
    - What part of SOX would apply to an IT professional?
    - How can an individual verify that a publicly traded company is SOX-compliant?
    - What are the 11 titles of mandates and requirements for SOX compliance?

15. In your browser's address box, **type http://www.isaca.org/COBIT/Pages/default.aspx** to open the Information Systems Audit and Control Association's Control Objectives for Information and related Technology (COBIT) website.

FIGURE 6.5

Viewing ISACA's
COBIT website

16. **Review** the website to locate the following information:
    - What is COBIT?
    - How can COBIT help with regulatory compliance?

17. In your browser's address box, **type https://www.pcisecuritystandards.org/security_standards/index.php** to open the Payment Card Industry's Data Security Standard (PCI DSS) website.

FIGURE 6.6

Viewing PCI's DSS website

18. **Click** the **For Merchants link** in the top navigation menu.

19. **Review** the website to locate the following information:

- What are the PCI DSS compliance requirements?
- Which organizations should be PCI DSS compliant?
- What is the purpose of the PCI DSS Security Audit Procedures?
- What is the process for obtaining PCI DSS compliance?
- What are the PCI DSS auditing procedures?
- What are the three steps for adhering to the PCI DSS?
- How does VISA define the levels of PCI DSS compliance?

20. In your browser's address box, **type http://www.aicpa.org/INTERESTAREAS/INFORMATIONTECHNOLOGY/ RESOURCES/TRUSTSERVICES/Pages/default.aspx** to open the American Institute of CPA's (AICPA) Trust Services Principles and Criteria website.

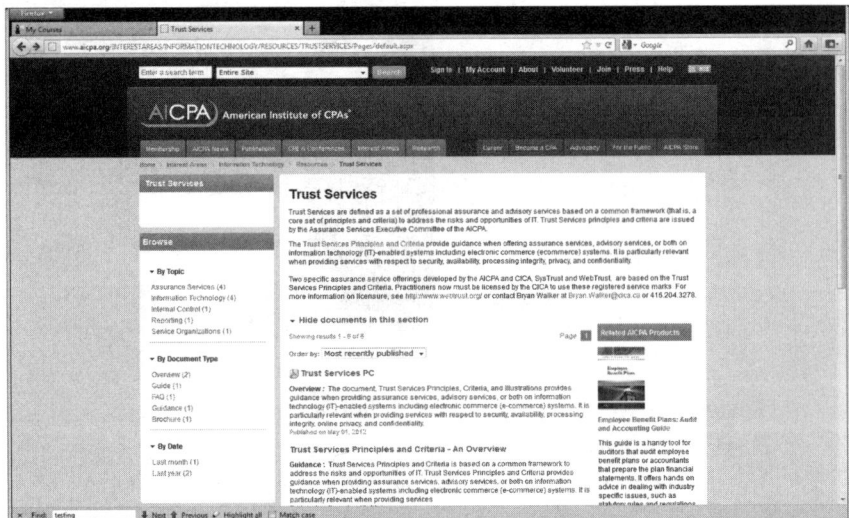

FIGURE 6.7

Viewing AICPA's Trust Services Principles and Criteria website

21. **Click** and **download** the **Trust Services PC link** in the center of the page and **save** the document to your workstation.

    This document is also available on the vWorkstation. **Use** the **File Transfer button** to download this file from the Security_Strategies folder (**C:\Security_Strategies\WebSecurity\item27805.pdf**).

22. **Review** the document to locate the following information:

    * What are the five principles of the Trust Services Principles and Criteria?
    * What aspects of the Trust Services Principles and Criteria impact websites?
    * What does the Trust Services Principles and Criteria recommend regarding inactive user accounts on a website?

23. **Complete** the following **Regulatory Compliance Matrix**. For each of the business examples in the first column, identify the appropriate regulation and/or industry compliance standard that governs it in the second column.

BUSINESS EXAMPLE	REGULATION/STANDARD
A publicly traded retailer with retail outlets and online shopping/shipping	
A city government that allows those with parking tickets to pay fines online using a credit card or online check	
A local residential cleaning business with a website that acts as a company brochure; no forms of any type are located on the website	
A regional health care organization, with 16 clinics, that shares patient information electronically over the Internet using VPN technologies	
A private, locally owned bank with a company website that accepts loan applications online	
A local doctor's office that keeps all patient information at the office, does not share electronically with anyone, doesn't have a website, and doesn't use any custom-developed software	
A software development company that develops and licenses online shopping software to large corporations	
An online-only retailer that sells athletic equipment, has shopping-cart software that has been developed in-house, and uses PayPal when a customer makes a purchase	

24. **Submit** the **Regulatory Compliance Matrix** to your instructor as a deliverable for this lab.
25. **Complete** the following **Organizational Compliance Table**. For each of the regulations and/or industry compliance standards in the center column, identify a business type or organization in the first column that would be governed by it. In the final column, give an explanation for your answer.

ORGANIZATION	REGULATORY OR INDUSTRY STANDARD	REASON/EXPLANATION
	FISMA	
	PCI DSS Only	
	HIPAA	
	GLBA	
	SOX	
	GLBA and PCI DSS	

26. **Submit** the **Organizational Compliance Table** to your instructor as a deliverable for this lab.
27. **Close** the **browser window**.

Evaluation Criteria and Rubrics

The following are the evaluation criteria and rubrics for Lab #6 that students must perform:

1. Was the student able to identify the criteria for compliance with the Health Insurance Portability and Accountability Act (HIPAA)? – [**15%**]

2. Was the student able to recognize secure software concepts for federal agencies using the Federal Information Security Management Act (FISMA) Implementation Project? – [**15%**]

3. Was the student able to identify the security control requirements for the Gramm-Leach-Bliley Act (GLBA) as it pertains to financial institutions? – [**15%**]

4. Was the student able to determine which organizations must comply with the Sarbanes-Oxley Act (SOX)? – [**15%**]

5. Was the student able to recognize when a business must comply with the Payment Card Industry Data Security Standard (PCI DSS)? – [**15%**]

6. Was the student able to review and assess how the American Institute of Certified Public Accountants (AICPA) standardizes the evaluation of consumer privacy during audits with "Trust Services"? – [**25%**]

LAB #6 – ASSESSMENT WORKSHEET

Align Compliance Requirements to HIPAA, FISMA, GLBA, SOX, PCI DSS, and AICPA

Course Name and Number:

Student Name:

Instructor Name:

Lab Due Date:

Overview

In this lab, you reviewed HIPAA, FISMA, GLBA, SOX, and PCI DSS. You also discovered how to classify an organization for compliance. Finally, you reviewed the purpose of the AICPA "Trust Services" as they relate to personal privacy.

Lab Assessment Questions & Answers

1. What are the five principles of the AICPA Trust Services Principles and Criteria?

2. What does the AICPA Trust Services Principles and Criteria recommend concerning inactive user accounts on a website?

3. With what section of SOX would the IT professional deal the most, and why?

4. Under HIPAA, when is a health care provider required to notify all patients and the Department of Health and Human Services when a security breach is discovered?

_____

_____

_____

_____

5. Where would someone go to find the quarterly and annual reports for a publicly traded company to verify SOX compliance?

_____

_____

_____

_____

6. Describe the various levels of PCI DSS compliance as defined by VISA.

_____

_____

_____

_____

_____

_____

_____

_____

7. Under HIPAA's Security Rule, what information is protected and who is covered?

_____

_____

_____

_____

_____

_____

_____

8. For the 12 core requirements of the PCI DSS standard, what are the three steps or phases for assessing and reviewing compliance with the PCI DSS standard?

_____

_____

_____

_____

9. What are the fines associated with violating HIPAA compliance requirements?

_____

_____

_____

_____

10. What are the PCI DSS procedures used when auditing an organization for security?

_____

_____

_____

_____

11. What are the 11 titles of mandates and requirements for SOX compliance?

_____

_____

_____

_____

_____

_____

_____

12. What purpose may COBIT serve to help comply with regulations such as Sarbanes-Oxley?

_____

_____

_____

_____

13. What is the Safeguards Rule as it relates to GLBA?

_____

_____

_____

_____

14. What is the purpose of the PCI Security Audit Procedures?

_____

_____

_____

_____

15. Describe the process to obtain/maintain PCI DSS compliance.

_____

_____

_____

_____

Perform Dynamic and Static Quality Control Testing

Introduction

In this lab, you will use dynamic testing techniques to identify vulnerabilities in Web application code. You also will perform static analysis testing on a source code file to identify exactly where the software code became more vulnerable. Finally, you will compare and analyze the Web application source code using skipfish and RATS commands to identify insecure coding tactics.

Learning Objectives

Upon completing this lab, you will be able to:

- Identify tools and techniques commonly used for website and Web application software code testing
- Use various techniques and tools to help provide the most comprehensive testing for software code and Web applications
- Dynamically test software for vulnerabilities in the code and understand the concepts and benefits of manual code reviews using the open source tool skipfish
- Perform static analysis testing on software source code and evaluate the advantages and disadvantages of various testing methods
- Compare and analyze the Web application source code using skipfish and RATS to help identify vulnerabilities and insecure coding tactics

TOOLS AND SOFTWARE	
NAME	**MORE INFORMATION**
Damn Vulnerable Web Application (DVWA)	http://www.dvwa.co.uk/
PuTTY	http://www.chiark.greenend.org.uk/~sgtatham/putty/
RATS	http://www.hpenterprisesecurity.com/products/hp-fortify-software-security-center/
skipfish	http://code.google.com/p/skipfish/

Deliverables

Upon completion of this lab, you are required to provide the following deliverables to your instructor:

1. skipfish.htm;
2. rats.html;
3. Lab Assessment Questions & Answers for Lab #7.

Hands-On Steps

1. This lab begins at the student landing vWorkstation virtual machine desktop of the VSCL, as shown here.

FIGURE 7.1

"Student Landing" VSCL workstation

> **Note:**
> The next steps will use SSH to connect to the lab's Web server, TargetUbuntu01. Once connected, you will disable the login authentication requirement for the Damn Vulnerable Web Application (DVWA) so that skipfish will be able to scan the application for vulnerabilities.

2. **Double-click** the **PuTTY icon** on the desktop to open the PuTTY application.

   PuTTY is a free utility that can open secure remote connections over the Internet via Telnet or SSH (secure shell).

3. In the PuTTY application window, **type** the IP address for the TargetUbuntu01 server, **172.30.0.4**. **Select** the **SSH radio button** and **click** the **Open button** to start the connection.

FIGURE 7.2

Using PuTTY to connect to TargetUbuntu01

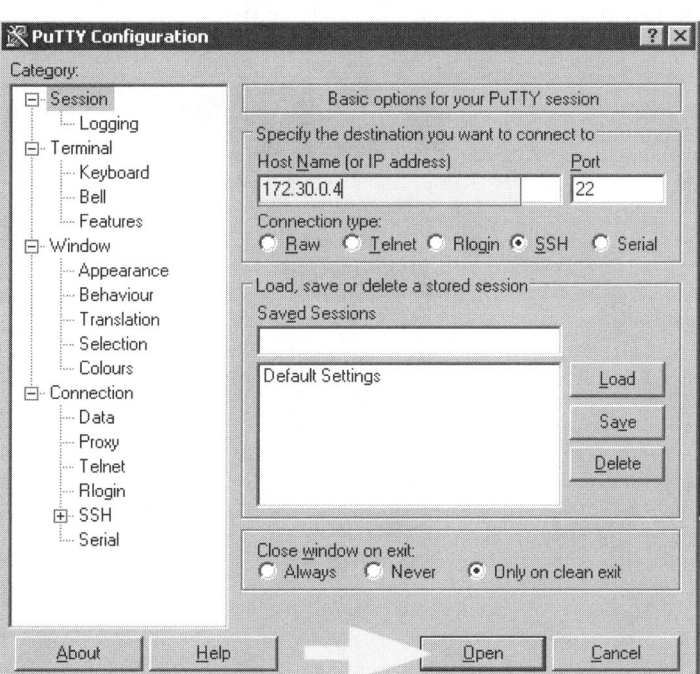

4. PuTTY will launch a terminal console window. At the login prompt, **type** the following credentials:
   - Username: **student**
   - Password: **ISS316Security**

FIGURE 7.3

PuTTY terminal console window

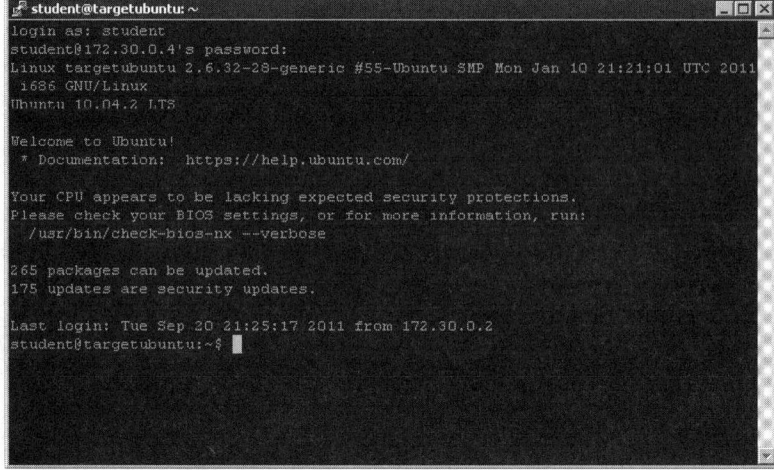

5. At the command prompt, **type sudo sed -i 's#dvwaRedirect(DVWA_WEB_PAGE_TO_ROOT.# //noauth #' /var/www/html/dvwa/dvwa/includes/dvwaPage.inc.php** and **press Enter** to disable the login authentication for the DVWA.
6. When prompted for the sudo password, **type ISS316Security**.
7. **Minimize** the **PuTTY terminal window**.
8. **Double-click** the **Mozilla Firefox icon** on the desktop to open the Firefox browser.

   You can access the DVWA tool using any Internet browser, but the steps in this lab will use the Firefox browser.
9. In the browser's address box, **type http://172.30.0.4/dvwa** and **press Enter** to open the Damn Vulnerable Web Application's Welcome page, bypassing the login screen. If you reach the login screen, maximize the PuTTY terminal window and repeat steps 5-9.

   DVWA is a Web application that is made purposefully vulnerable. It is installed on a local Web server to allow security analysts a safe place to test the security of their applications.

FIGURE 7.4

DVWA Welcome page

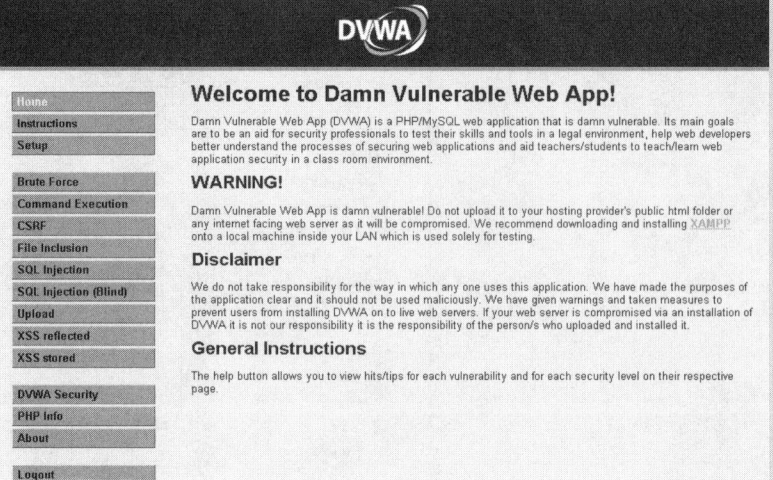

10. **Maximize** the **PuTTY terminal window**.

> **Note:**
> The next steps will use skipfish to perform a dynamic scan for vulnerabilities on the DVWA. You will review the skipfish report and save a copy to submit to your instructor as a deliverable for this lab.

11. At the command prompt, **type sudo skipfish -I "dvwa" -W /dev/null -b i -o /var/www/html/scan -C "security=low" -C "PHPSESSID=1234test" -r 50000 http://localhost/dvwa/vulnerabilities** and **press Enter** to start a skipfish scan which will send 50,000 requests to the DVWA website and write an HTML version of the report in a new directory (scan).

    This scan takes several minutes and the terminal window will display the progress throughout the scan. The reappearance of the command prompt indicates that the scan is complete.

FIGURE 7.5

Skipfish vulnerability
scan completed

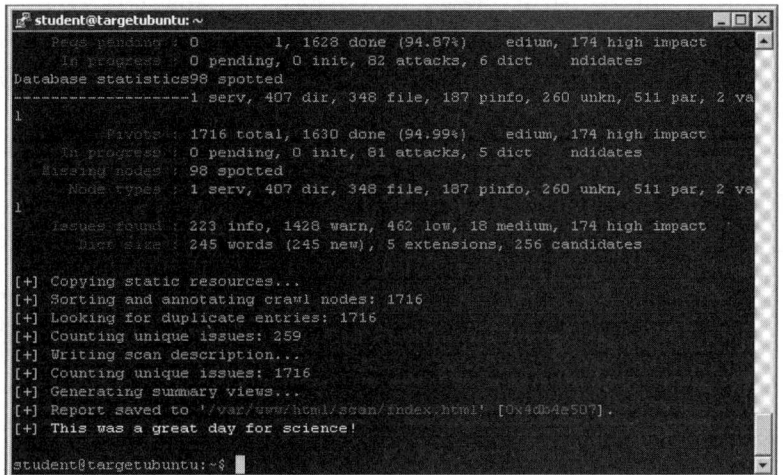

12. **Minimize** the **PuTTY terminal window**.
13. **Open** a **new tab** in the browser and **type http://172.30.0.4/scan** in the browser's address box to open the scan directory created by skipfish.

FIGURE 7.6

Viewing the skipfish
report

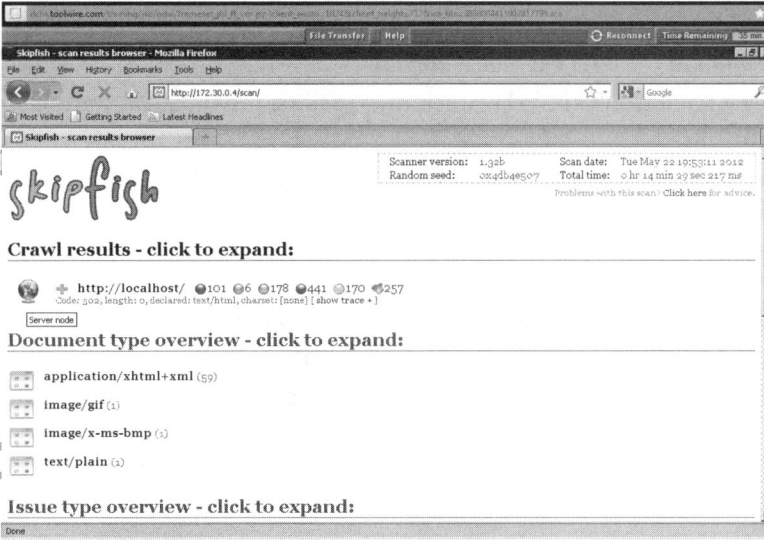

14. In the browser's menu, **click File > Save Page As. Click** the **Desktop button, select Web Page, complete** from the Save as type drop-down menu, and **type skipfish** in the File name box to save the report to the vWorkstation desktop.

> **Note:**
> The next steps will use RATS (Rough Auditing Tool for Security), part of the HP Fortify Software Security Center. You will use RATS commands to perform a static analysis scan on the DVWA source code. You will review the RATS report and save a copy to submit to your instructor as a deliverable for this lab.

15. **Maximize** the **PuTTY terminal window**.

16. At the command prompt, type **sudo rats - -html /var/www/html/dvwa > /home/student/rats.html** to start the RATS scan.

    RATS is a free tool that scans source code and flags common security-related programming errors, such as buffer overflows. This command will scan the DVWA source code and write a report to the student directory.

17. At the command prompt, **type sudo cp /home/student/rats.html /var/www/html/rats.html** and **press Enter** to copy the RATS report to the Web application directory (html).

FIGURE 7.7

Executing RATS static analysis tool on TargetUbuntu01 VM

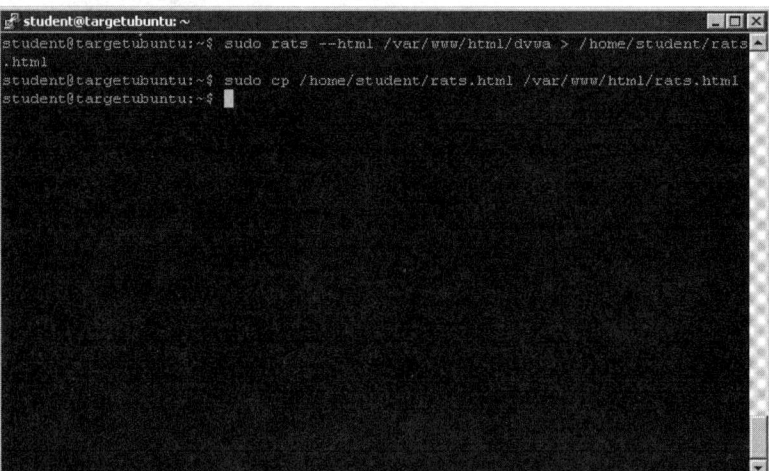

18. **Minimize** the **PuTTY terminal window**.

19. Open a new tab in the browser and **type http://172.30.0.4/rats.html** in the browser's address box to open the report.

20. In the browser's menu, **click File > Save Page As. Click** the **Desktop button, select Web Page, complete** from the Save as type drop-down menu, and **type rats** in the File name box to save the report to the vWorkstation desktop.

21. **Maximize** the **PuTTY terminal window**.

22. At the command prompt, **type cd /var/www/html/dvwa/vulnerabilities/xss_r/source** and **press Enter** to change the directory to the source code for DVWA's XSS_r (reflected cross-site scripting) tests.

23. At the command prompt, **type ls** and **press Enter** to list the files in that directory.

    The system should display three files: high.php, medium.php, and low.php. These files contain the source code for the XSS tests when the DVWA security is set to high, medium, or low.

24. At the command prompt, **type vi -o high.php low.php** and **press Enter twice** to open both files in a split frame on the terminal window.

FIGURE 7.8

Viewing files in a
split view

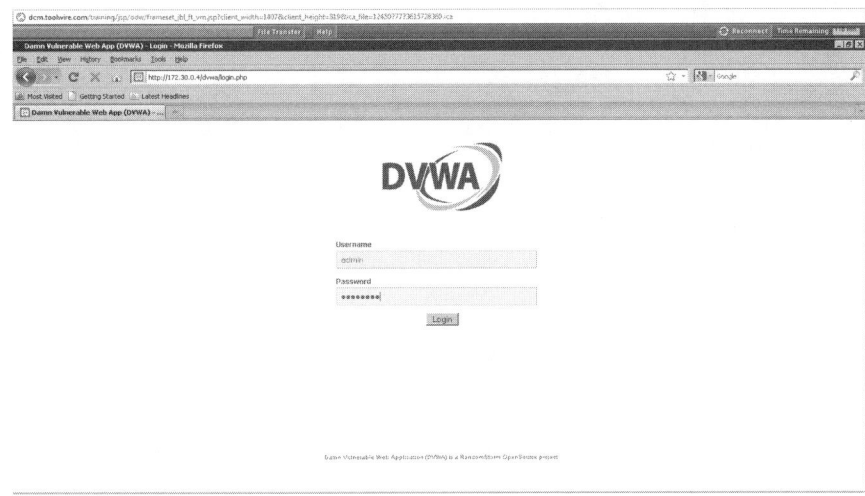

25. **Review** the files and make note of the differences in the source code for these two security levels. You will need this information for the deliverables in this lab.

   To review the files in the vi editor, **use** the **arrow keys** within each pane to read the file. To switch between panes, **hold Ctrl** and **press W** and **press** the **arrow key** (up or down) that corresponds to the location of the pane that you want to read.

26. **Hold Ctrl** and **press Z** to exit the vi editor and return to the command prompt.

27. At the command prompt, **type sudo sed -i 's# //noauth # dvwaRedirect(DVWA_WEB_PAGE_TO_ROOT. #' /var/www/html/dvwa/dvwa/includes/dvwaPage.inc.php** and **press Enter** to re-enable the login authentication for DVWA.

28. If prompted for the sudo password, **type ISS316Security**.

29. **Minimize** the **PuTTY terminal window**.

30. In the browser, **click** the **DVWA tab** and **click** the browser's **Refresh button** to reload the Damn Vulnerable Web Application.

   The DVWA should open to the login screen indicating that the login authentication has been re-enabled for this application. If you do not see this login screen, maximize the PuTTY terminal window and repeat steps 27-30.

FIGURE 7.9

DVWA login screen

7

Perform Dynamic and Static
Quality Control Testing

31. **Log in** to the application with the following credentials and **click Login** to verify that the authentication has been restored properly:
    * Username: **admin**
    * Password: **password**

    The DVWA should open the Welcome screen.

32. **Close** the **Mozilla Firefox window**.

    If prompted to save the Firefox tabs, **click** the **Quit button**.

33. **Close** the **PuTTY terminal window**.

34. Use the **File Transfer button** to **download** the two reports generated by this lab: **skipfish.htm** (and the related files in the **Skipfish_files folder**) and **rats.html**, and **submit** them to your instructor as part of your deliverables for this lab.

35. **Keep** these **files** for your own records; you will use them again in Lab #8.

Evaluation Criteria and Rubrics

The following are the evaluation criteria and rubrics for Lab #7 that students must perform:

1. Was the student able to identify tools and techniques commonly used for website and Web application software code testing? – **[20%]**

2. Was the student able to use various techniques and tools to help provide the most comprehensive testing for software code and Web applications? – **[20%]**

3. Was the student able to dynamically test software for vulnerabilities in the code and to understand the concepts and benefits of manual code reviews using the open source tool skipfish? – **[20%]**

4. Was the student able to perform static analysis testing on software source code and evaluate the advantages and disadvantages of various testing methods? – **[20%]**

5. Was the student able to compare and analyze Web application source code using skipfish and RATS to help determine vulnerabilities and insecure coding tactics? – **[20%]**

LAB #7 – ASSESSMENT WORKSHEET

Perform Dynamic and Static Quality Control Testing

Course Name and Number:

_____

Student Name:

_____

Instructor Name:

_____

Lab Due Date:

_____

Overview

In this lab, you used dynamic testing techniques to identify vulnerabilities in Web application code. You also performed static analysis testing on a source code file to identify exactly where the software code became more vulnerable. Finally, you compared and analyzed the Web application source code using skipfish and RATS commands to identify insecure coding tactics.

Lab Assessment Questions & Answers

1. How does skipfish categorize findings in the scan report?

_____

_____

_____

_____

_____

2. Which tool used in the lab is considered a static analysis tool? Explain what is referred to by static code analysis.

_____

_____

_____

_____

3. What possible high-risk vulnerabilities did the RATS tool find in the DVWA application source code?

_____

_____

_____

_____

4. Did the static analysis tool find all of the potential security flaws in the application?

_____

_____

_____

_____

5. What is black-box testing on a website or Web application?

_____

_____

_____

_____

6. Explain the skipfish command in detail: : **./skipfish -o /var/scans/is308lab.org -A admin:password -d 3 -b i -X logout.jsp -r 200000 http://www.is308lab.org**

_____

_____

_____

_____

7. During the manual code review, what do you notice about high.php that makes it less likely to victimize users with XSS reflection, and why is it considered more secure?

_____

_____

_____

_____

_____

_____

8. Would Firefox be considered a Web application assessment tool?

_____

_____

_____

_____

9. Compare and contrast a penetration-testing tool such as OWASP WebScarab with an automatic analysis tool like skipfish.

_____

_____

_____

_____

_____

_____

10. Judging from the two scan reports, describe how skipfish and RATS can complement each other.

_____

_____

_____

_____

_____

Perform an IT and Web Application Security Assessment

Introduction

In this lab, you will apply the research you conducted in Lab #5 and the security scans you performed in Lab #7. You will analyze the skipfish and RATS reports you saved from Lab #7 to identify the website and Web application security issues, as well as software code vulnerabilities found in the Damn Vulnerable Web Application (DVWA). You also will relate your research findings from Lab #5 to map those vulnerabilities to specific remediation and best practice recommendations based on the OWASP and OpenSAMM models. Finally, you will use PowerPoint to create a Web Application Security Assessment presentation of your work in this lab.

This lab is a paper-based design lab and does not require use of the Virtual Security Cloud Lab (VSCL). To successfully complete the deliverables for this lab, you will need access to a text editor or word processor, such as Microsoft® Word. For some labs, you may also need access to a graphics line drawing application, such as Visio or PowerPoint.

 Note:
If you don't have a word processor or graphics package, use OpenOffice on the student landing vWorkstation for your lab deliverables and to answer the lab assessment questions. To capture screenshots, **press Prt Sc > MSPAINT, paste** into a text document, and **save** the document in the Security_Strategies folder (**C:\Security_Strategies**) using the File Transfer function.

Learning Objectives

Upon completing this lab, you will be able to:

- Analyze reports from dynamic code analysis, and summarize your findings in an effort to get more secure testing and coding of Web applications
- Identify vulnerabilities in reports from dynamic code analysis, and make security recommendations on how to better harden the code
- Analyze reports from static code analysis, and summarize your findings in an effort to get more secure testing and coding of Web applications
- Identify vulnerabilities in reports from static code analysis, and make security recommendations on how to better harden the code
- Based on a website assessment, make remediation recommendations that include both your static and dynamic analyses of the Web application code

TOOLS AND SOFTWARE	
NAME	**MORE INFORMATION**
None	

Deliverables

Upon completion of this lab, you are required to provide the following deliverables to your instructor:

1. Web Application Security Assessment.ppt;
2. Lab Assessment Questions & Answers for Lab #8.

Hands-On Steps

1. This lab begins at a workstation with Internet access. **Double-click** any **Internet browser icon** on your desktop to open the application.

> **Note:**
> The next steps will analyze the skipfish.htm and rats.html reports you generated in Lab #7. You will use this analysis in a later step.

2. In your browser, **open** the **skipfish.htm report** that you saved in Lab #7 and **explore** the **results**.

Issue type overview - click to expand:

- ● **PUT request accepted** (88)
- ● **Integer overflow vector** (3)
- ● **Format string vector** (3)
- ● **SQL injection vector** (1)
- ● **Shell injection vector** (6)
- ● **Incorrect or missing charset (higher risk)** (4)
- ● **Incorrect or missing MIME type (higher risk)** (2)
- ● **HTML form with no apparent XSRF protection** (174)
- ● **Directory listing restrictions bypassed** (4)
- ● **Node should be a directory, detection error?** (12)
- ● **Response varies randomly, skipping injection checks** (121)
- ● **IPS filtering enabled** (81)
- ● **Behavior checks failed** (6)
- ● **Limits exceeded, fetch suppressed** (221)
- ○ **Numerical filename - consider enumerating** (29)
- ○ **Incorrect or missing MIME type (low risk)** (1)
- ○ **Password entry form - consider brute-force** (6)
- ○ **Unknown form field (can't autocomplete)** (1)
- ○ **New 404 signature seen** (127)
- ○ **New 'X-*' header value seen** (4)
- ○ **New 'Server' header value seen** (1)
- ○ **New HTTP cookie added** (1)

NOTE: 100 samples maximum per issue or document type.

3. In your browser's address box, **type google.com** to open the search tool. Use the search tool to **locate information about mitigations** for the risks skipfish reported.

4. In your browser, **open** the **rats.html report** that you saved in Lab #7 and **explore** the **results**.

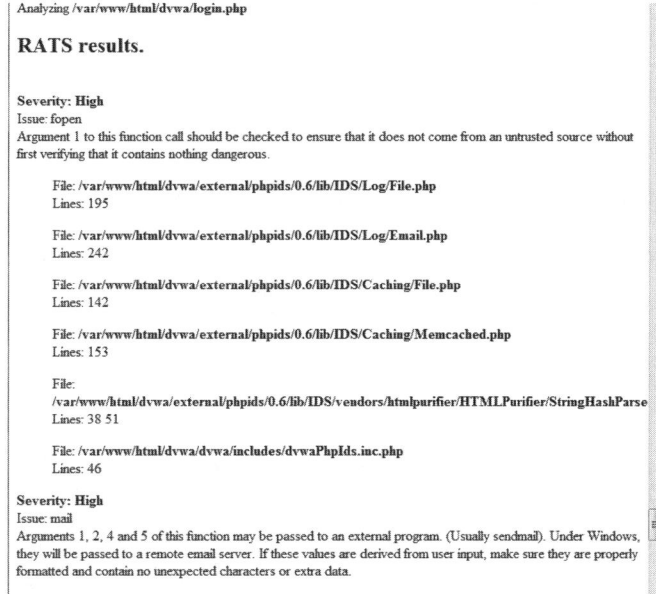

Analyzing /var/www/html/dvwa/login.php

RATS results.

Severity: High
Issue: fopen
Argument 1 to this function call should be checked to ensure that it does not come from an untrusted source without first verifying that it contains nothing dangerous.

    File: /var/www/html/dvwa/external/phpids/0.6/lib/IDS/Log/File.php
    Lines: 195

    File: /var/www/html/dvwa/external/phpids/0.6/lib/IDS/Log/Email.php
    Lines: 242

    File: /var/www/html/dvwa/external/phpids/0.6/lib/IDS/Caching/File.php
    Lines: 142

    File: /var/www/html/dvwa/external/phpids/0.6/lib/IDS/Caching/Memcached.php
    Lines: 153

    File:
    /var/www/html/dvwa/external/phpids/0.6/lib/IDS/vendors/htmlpurifier/HTMLPurifier/StringHashParse
    Lines: 38 51

    File: /var/www/html/dvwa/dvwa/includes/dvwaPhpIds.inc.php
    Lines: 46

Severity: High
Issue: mail
Arguments 1, 2, 4 and 5 of this function may be passed to an external program. (Usually sendmail). Under Windows, they will be passed to a remote email server. If these values are derived from user input, make sure they are properly formatted and contain no unexpected characters or extra data.

5. Use the Google search tool to **locate information about mitigations** for the high severity risks identified by the RATS report.

 Note:
The next steps will create the Web Application Security Assessment presentation. You will need this presentation as a deliverable for this lab.

6. **Review** the **testing research** you downloaded in Lab #5:
   * **Software Assurance Maturity Model** (SAMM-1.0.pdf)
   * **OWASP Application Security Verification Standard** (OWASP_ASVS_2009_Web_App_Std_Release.pdf)
   * **OWASP Development Guide** (OWASPGuide2.0.1.pdf)
   * **OWASP Code Review Guide** (OWASP_Code_Review_Guide-V1_1.pdf)
   * **OWASP Testing Guide** (OWASP_Testing_Guide_v3.pdf)

   If you do not have a copy of the documents that you downloaded during the lab, you can **use** the **File Transfer button** on the vWorkstation to download them from the Security_Strategies folder (**C:\Security_Strategies\WebSecurity**).

7. From your workstation, **click File > All Programs > Microsoft® Office** and **select Microsoft® PowerPoint** from the menu.

8. **Create** a new **Web Application Security Assessment presentation** that illustrates your analysis of the vulnerabilities of the DVWA. The presentation should include the following outline:
   * Cover page (include your name and a title)
   * Executive Summary (include a general overview of the security state of the DVWA)
   * Summary of Methods/Tools Used
   * Summary of Findings (include at least 10 vulnerabilities and classify them as high, medium, or low risk)
   * Recommendations (map the vulnerabilities from the previous section to specific remediation/ best practice recommendations outlined by the OWASP and OpenSAMM models; cite your work properly)

9. **Close** the **browser window**.

10. **Submit** the **Web Application Security Assessment** to your instructor as a deliverable for this lab.

Evaluation Criteria and Rubrics

The following are the evaluation criteria and rubrics for Lab #8 that students must perform:

1. Was the student able to analyze reports from dynamic code analysis and summarize his/her findings in an effort to get more secure testing and coding of Web applications? – [**20%**]

2. Was the student able to identify vulnerabilities in reports from dynamic code analysis and make security recommendations on how to better harden the code? – [**20%**]

3. Was the student able to analyze reports from static code analysis and summarize his/her findings in an effort to get more secure testing and coding of Web applications? – [**20%**]

4. Was the student able to identify vulnerabilities in reports from static code analysis and make security recommendations on how to better harden the code? – [**20%**]

5. Was the student able to make remediation recommendations, based on a website assessment, that include both the student's static and dynamic analyses of the Web application code? – [**20%**]

LAB #8 – ASSESSMENT WORKSHEET

Perform an IT and Web Application Security Assessment

Course Name and Number:

_____

Student Name:

_____

Instructor Name:

_____

Lab Due Date:

_____

Overview

In this lab, you applied the research you conducted in Lab #5 and the security scans you performed in Lab #7. You analyzed the skipfish and RATS reports you saved from Lab #7 to identify the website and Web application security issues, as well as software code vulnerabilities found in the Damn Vulnerable Web Application (DVWA). You also related your research findings from Lab #5 to map those vulnerabilities to specific remediation and best practice recommendations based on the OWASP and OpenSAMM models. Finally, you used PowerPoint to create a Web Application Security Assessment presentation of your work in this lab.

Lab Assessment Questions & Answers

1. Once an organization has identified a known vulnerability, what recourse does the company have?

_____

_____

_____

_____

2. If an application has a known vulnerability that is reported, how should a company proceed?

_____

_____

_____

_____

3. Name two network entry points as they pertain to network accessibility.

_____

_____

_____

4. What types of authentication and authorization requirements should be audited in a vulnerability assessment?

_____

_____

_____

_____

5. When categorizing vulnerabilities for a report that enumerates them, what model should an auditor use?

_____

_____

_____

_____

6. What is the standard formula used to rank potential threats?

_____

_____

_____

_____

7. If an organization were identified as not having any password policies for any of its applications, what would be two suggestions to note in the assessment?

_____

_____

_____

_____

8. Should newly released patches for a known vulnerability be applied to production systems once released?

_____

_____

_____

_____

9. What is the importance of having a security-incident response plan in an organization?

_____

_____

_____

_____

10. What would an auditor be trying to verify if he/she is asking to view logs for certain dates?

_____

_____

_____

_____

11. How could the findings from the skipfish and RATS scanning performed in Lab #7 be categorized and presented in an assessment report?

_____

_____

_____

_____

12. Assume the analysis tool skipfish used in Lab #7 is to be included in a Web assessment report. What pertinent information about the method of testing and the tools used could an auditor include in an assessment report?

_____

_____

_____

_____

13. Provide a remediation recommendation for a potential vulnerability found using the "eval" function in a static analysis report.

_____

_____

_____

14. Explain the process for remediating an XSS scripting vulnerability found by a dynamic analysis tool.

_____

_____

_____

_____

15. Why is client-side validation not considered a secure way to prevent SQL injection?

_____

_____

_____

_____

Recognize Risks and Threats Associated with Social Networking and Mobile Communications

Introduction

In this lab, you will research the risks, threats, and vulnerabilities inherent with cloud computing, social networking, and mobile applications. You will create a Risks and Threats of Social Networking and Mobile Communications Research Report with a summary of your findings. You also will complete a Risk Assessment Table identifying the top three risks for each of these technologies.

This lab is a paper-based design lab and does not require use of the Virtual Security Cloud Lab (VSCL). To successfully complete the deliverables for this lab, you will need access to a text editor or word processor, such as Microsoft® Word. For some labs, you may also need access to a graphics line drawing application, such as Visio or PowerPoint.

 Note:
If you don't have a word processor or graphics package, use OpenOffice on the student landing vWorkstation for your lab deliverables and to answer the lab assessment questions. To capture screenshots, **press Prt Sc > MSPAINT, paste** into a text document, and **save** the document in the Security_Strategies folder (**C:\Security_Strategies**) using the File Transfer function.

Learning Objectives

Upon completing this lab, you will be able to:

- Recognize the risks that social networking and peer-to-peer sites could introduce into an organization, and recommend hardening techniques to minimize exposure
- Evaluate the risks associated with using mobile devices in an organization by analyzing all possible vectors and using best practices to mitigate the risks
- Evaluate and recognize the security advantages and disadvantages of cloud and grid computing
- Apply industry-specific best practices provided by the Cloud Security Alliance (CSA) and the European Network and Information Security Agency (ENISA) to recognize and evaluate risk in cloud and grid computing
- Provide written analysis regarding hot security topics in emerging technologies, and create a strategy to maintain situational awareness of new security risks

TOOLS AND SOFTWARE	
NAME	**MORE INFORMATION**
None	

Deliverables

Upon completion of this lab, you are required to provide the following deliverables to your instructor:

1. Risks and Threats of Social Networking and Mobile Communications Research Report;
2. Lab Assessment Questions & Answers for Lab #9.

Hands-On Steps

1. This lab begins at a workstation with Internet access. **Double-click** any **Internet browser icon** on your desktop to open the application.

> **Note:**
>
> The next steps will conduct Internet research surrounding the risks and threats associated with several emerging technologies. You will summarize your research in a Risks and Threats of Social Networking and Mobile Communications Research Report.

2. In a new text document, **create** a **Risks and Threats of Social Networking and Mobile Communications Research Report**.

   You will be responsible for determining what to document in this report based on your summary of each of the documents you will review as part of this lab.

3. In your browser's address box, **type http://csrc.nist.gov/publications/nistpubs/800-145/SP800-145.pdf** to open the National Institute of Standards and Technology (NIST) Definition of Cloud Computing.

FIGURE 9.1

Viewing the NIST
Definition of Cloud
Computing

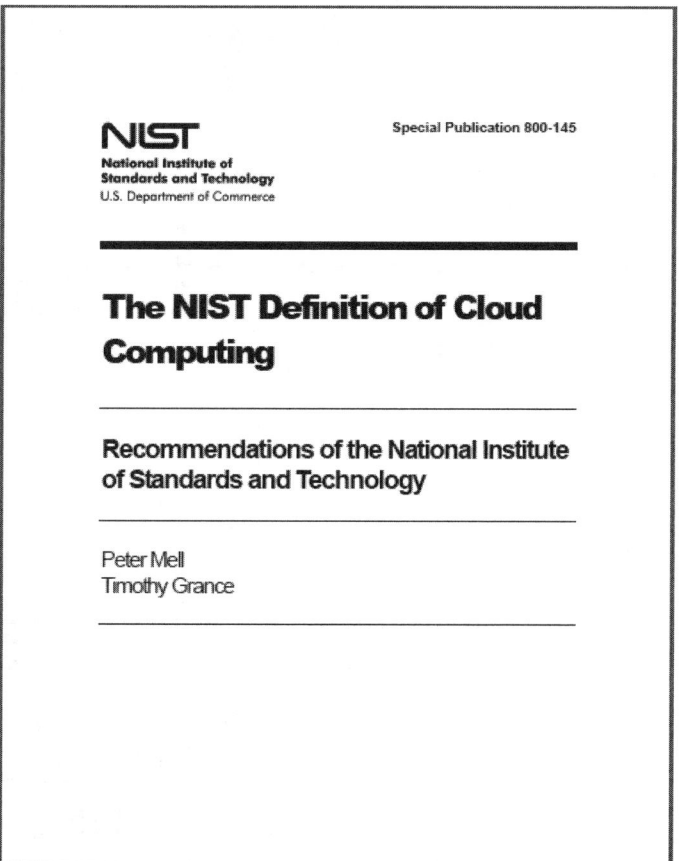

4. **Review** the document for a general overview of cloud computing and **locate** the following information:
   * What are the three cloud service models?
   * What are the four deployment models of cloud computing?

5. In your browser's address box, **type http://aws.amazon.com/ec2** to open the Amazon Elastic Compute Cloud website and **read** the EC2 Overview page to find out about this cloud option.

6. **Click** the **EC2 FAQs link** in the left navigation menu and **review** the answers to the set of questions under the General category.

7. In your browser's address box, **type http://www.cloudsecurityalliance.org** to open the CSA's website.

8. **Click Research** in the top navigation bar and **select Security Guidance** from the menu.

9. **Click** the **Download (pdf) link** in the Document: Security Guidance section of the page.

   You will see a pop-up window with a Guidance V3 button and a questionnaire.

Viewing the CSA document pop-up window

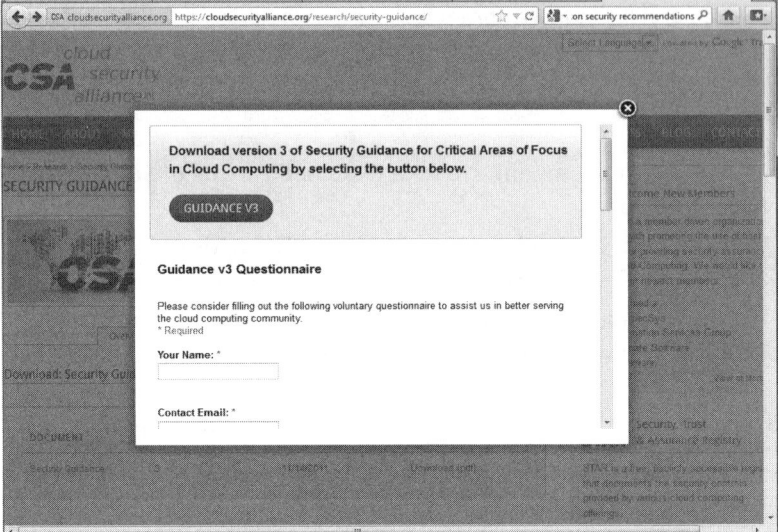

10. **Click** the **Guidance V3 button** to open the PDF version of the Security Guidance for Critical Areas of Focus in Cloud Computing.

Viewing the CSA's Security Guidance

11. **Review** the document and **locate** the following information:
    - How many domains of cloud security are there? Briefly describe each.
    - What are the categories that CSA uses to classify the cloud domains? Briefly describe each.
    - What are some best practices an organization should require of its cloud provider?
    - What should an organization expect of its cloud provider's incident-response plan?

12. In your browser's address box, **type http://www.enisa.europa.eu** to open the European Network and Information Security Agency's website.

FIGURE 9.4

Viewing the ENISA website

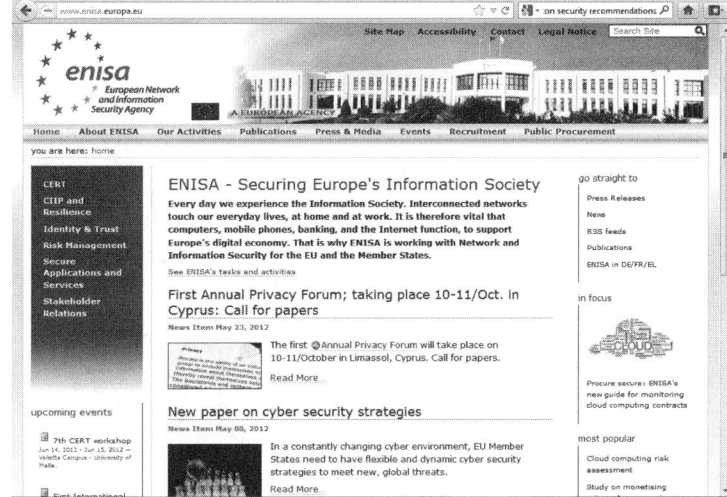

13. **Click** the **Cloud computing risk assessment link** in the most popular section of the right navigation box.

14. From the Downloads section of the page, **click** the **PDF link**, in your preferred language, and **open** the Cloud Computing Security Risk Assessment document.

FIGURE 9.5

Viewing the ENISA Cloud Computing document

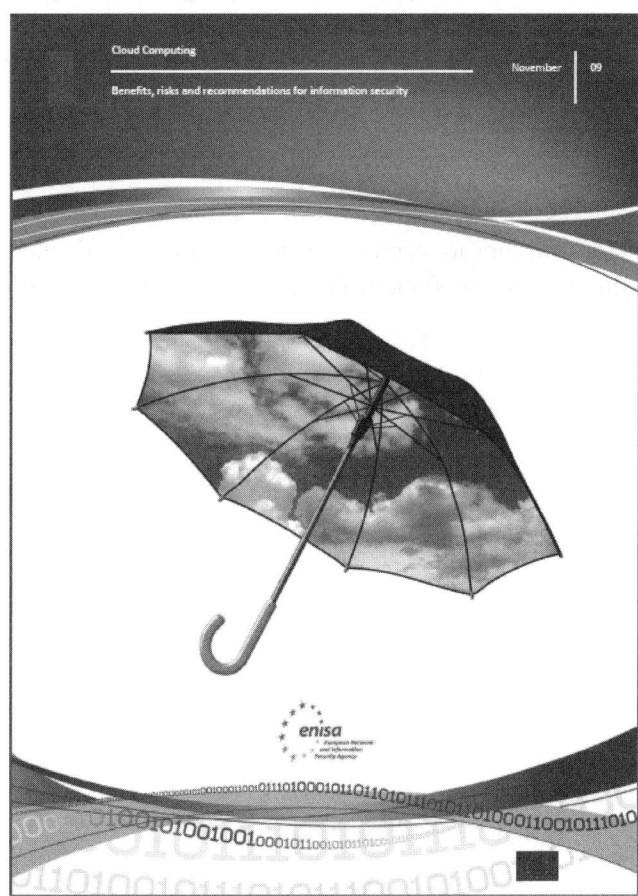

15. **Review** the document and **locate** the following information:
    - What are four security risks in using cloud computing?
    - What are four legal risks that are common across all cloud-computing scenarios?
    - What are four security checklist recommendations for potential cloud customers?
16. **Close** the **Adobe Reader window**.
17. **Review** the following diagram. Based on the research you have already done in this lab, **briefly describe** each of the risks for cloud computing.

FIGURE 9.6

Risks in cloud computing

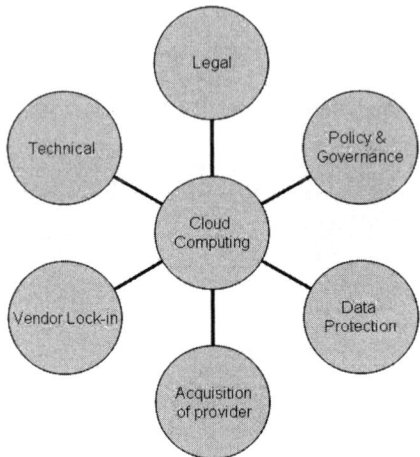

18. In your browser's address box, **type http://www.google.com** to open the search tool and research each of the following topics:
    - What are some ways to protect the physical security of a corporate mobile device or laptop while traveling?
    - What are risks associated with flash drives?
    - What are risks associated with using a service such as dropbox.com?
19. In your research report, **answer** the following questions:
    - What are pros and cons for each of the cloud computing deployment models?
    - What are three recommendations for cloud application security in the future?

20. Using your research, **complete** the following **Risk Assessment Table** by identifying the top three threats associated with each of these technologies. For any threat with a ranking of medium or high, provide a recommended control to help mitigate the risk. For any low-ranking risk, provide a note explaining why the risk is considered low.

EMERGING TECHNOLOGY CLASSIFICATION	IDENTIFIED THREATS	RISK IMPACT (CRITICAL, MAJOR, MINOR)	RECOMMENDED SECURITY CONTROL	NOTES
Cloud Computing				
Cloud Computing				
Cloud Computing				
Mobile Devices				
Mobile Devices				
Mobile Devices				
Social Networking				
Social Networking				
Social Networking				

21. **Close** the **browser window**.
22. **Submit** the **Risks and Threats of Social Networking and Mobile Communications Research Report** to your instructor as a deliverable for this lab.

Evaluation Criteria and Rubrics

The following are the evaluation criteria and rubrics for Lab #9 that students must perform:

1. Was the student able to recognize the risks that social networking and peer-to-peer sites could introduce into an organization and recommend hardening techniques to minimize exposure? – [**20%**]

2. Was the student able to evaluate the risks associated with using mobile devices in an organization by analyzing all possible vectors and using best practices to mitigate the risks? – [**20%**]

3. Was the student able to evaluate and recognize the security advantages and disadvantages of cloud and grid computing? – [**20%**]

4. Was the student able to apply industry-specific best practices provided by the Cloud Security Alliance (CSA) and the European Network and Information Security Agency (ENISA) to recognize and evaluate risk in cloud and grid computing? – [**20%**]

5. Was the student able to provide written analysis regarding hot security topics in emerging technologies and create a strategy to maintain situational awareness of new security risks? – [**20%**]

LAB #9 – ASSESSMENT WORKSHEET

Recognize Risks and Threats Associated with Social Networking and Mobile Communications

Course Name and Number:
_____

Student Name:
_____

Instructor Name:
_____

Lab Due Date:
_____

Overview

In this lab, you researched the risks, threats, and vulnerabilities inherent with cloud computing, social networking, and mobile applications. You created a Risks and Threats of Social Networking and Mobile Communications Research Report with a summary of your findings. You also completed a Risk Assessment Table identifying the top three risks for each of these technologies.

Lab Assessment Questions & Answers

1. What are the four security checklist recommendations from the ENISA guide that customers who want to obtain cloud services should use?

_____

_____

_____

_____

_____

_____

_____

2. Name five cloud security domains according to the CSA guide. How many are there in total?

_____

_____

_____

_____

_____

_____

_____

_____

_____

_____

3. What three cloud service models are primarily available for customers today?

_____

_____

_____

_____

4. What four deployment models are there for cloud services regardless of the deliverable service models?

_____

_____

_____

_____

5. For an organization to understand the incident-response plan from a cloud perspective, what must the strategy entail?

_____

_____

_____

_____

6. Name four security risks in using cloud computing as per the ENISA guide.

_____

_____

_____

_____

7. What are four legal issues that are common across all cloud-computing scenarios?

_____

_____

_____

_____

8. What are three recommendations for cloud application security in the future?

_____

_____

_____

_____

9. What are the two broad categories that the CSA's Security Guidance uses to classify the cloud domains?

_____

_____

_____

_____

10. When traveling with a corporate mobile device, what are some ways to help protect the device's physical security?

_____

_____

_____

_____

11. What are pros and cons of some of the popular cloud-computing deployment models?

_____

_____

_____

_____

12. What are some unique risks that flash or portable hard drives present to organizations? How can the risks be mitigated?

_____

_____

_____

_____

13. What are the risks associated with an employee using a service such as dropbox.com to maintain and share company files? How should the risks be approached?

_____

_____

_____

_____

14. According to the Cloud Security Alliance guide, what are some security best practices an organization should have in place with the cloud provider before implementing a solution?

_____

_____

_____

_____

_____

15. Name two governance domains and three operational domains.

_____

_____

_____

_____

_____

_____

_____

_____

Build a Web Application and Security Development Life Cycle Plan

Introduction

In this lab, you will conduct research into the Microsoft® Security Development Lifecycle (SDL) and the traditional software development life cycle (SDLC). Using that research, you will draft a Security Development Life Cycle Plan for an Internet sales company, Online Goodies, which incorporates checkpoints for proper security testing and penetration testing for Web servers and Web applications.

This lab is a paper-based design lab and does not require use of the Virtual Security Cloud Lab (VSCL). To successfully complete the deliverables for this lab, you will need access to a text editor or word processor, such as Microsoft® Word. For some labs, you may also need access to a graphics line drawing application, such as Visio or PowerPoint.

> **Note:**
> If you don't have a word processor or graphics package, use OpenOffice on the student landing vWorkstation for your lab deliverables and to answer the lab assessment questions. To capture screenshots, **press Prt Sc > MSPAINT, paste** into a text document, and **save** the document in the Security_Strategies folder (**C:\Security_Strategies**) using the File Transfer function.

Learning Objectives

Upon completing this lab, you will be able to:

- Design a general security life cycle strategy for a Web application based on the software development life cycle (SDLC)
- Recognize how automated and manual processes can benefit a security life cycle strategy, mapping recommendations to best practices
- Identify the various roles when implementing a security life cycle strategy and assign these roles to individuals within an organization
- Integrate a compliance process into a security life cycle strategy, so that applications that must meet regulatory compliance are up to the standards required
- Identify appropriate tools for use in each phase of the software development life cycle for proper implementation of best practice guidelines

TOOLS AND SOFTWARE	
NAME	**MORE INFORMATION**
None	

Deliverables

Upon completion of this lab, you are required to provide the following deliverables to your instructor:

1. Security Development Life Cycle Plan;
2. Lab Assessment Questions & Answers for Lab #10.

Hands-On Steps

1. This lab begins at a workstation with Internet access. **Double-click** any **Internet browser icon** on your desktop to open the application.

> **Note:**
>
> The next steps will conduct Internet research on the Microsoft® Security Development Lifecycle (SDL) and the traditional software development life cycle (SDLC). You will use this information to complete the Lab Assessment Questions. You also will put your research in action when you create a Security Development Life Cycle Plan for Online Goodies.

2. In your browser's address box, **type http://www.microsoft.com/security/sdl/default.aspx** to open the Microsoft® SDL website.

FIGURE 10.1

Viewing the Microsoft®
SDL website

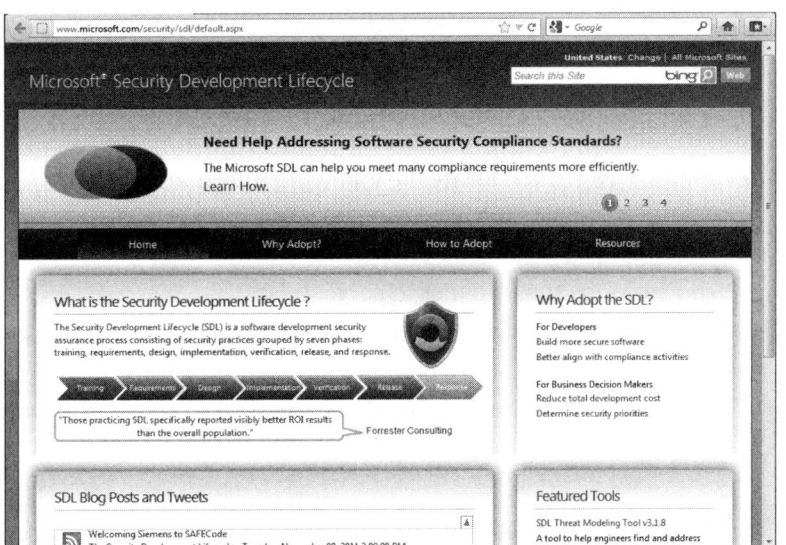

3. **Review** the website and **locate** the following information:
   - What are the elements of a successful SDL?
   - What are the activities that occur within each phase?
   - Who performs the activities in each phase?
   - What is STRIDE?

10

Build a Web Application and Security
Development Life Cycle Plan

4. In your browser's address box, **type http://www.waterfall-model.com/sdlc/** to learn about the traditional software development life cycle (SDLC).

The acronym SDLC is used interchangeably within the industry as either software development life cycle or systems development life cycle. In either case, it refers to the development of an information technology product.

FIGURE 10.2

Traditional SDLC

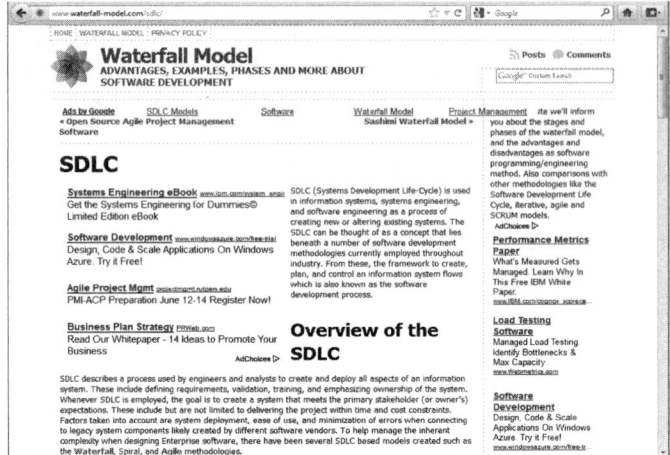

5. **Review** the website and **locate** the following information:
   - What are the elements of a successful SDLC?
   - What are the activities that occur within each phase?
   - Who performs the activities in each phase?

6. **Review** the following diagrams and respond to the following questions in your deliverables:
   - How do the two diagrams demonstrate that secure software doesn't happen by accident?
   - What role does accountability play in secure software development?

FIGURE 10.3

SDL and the Secure Coding Approach

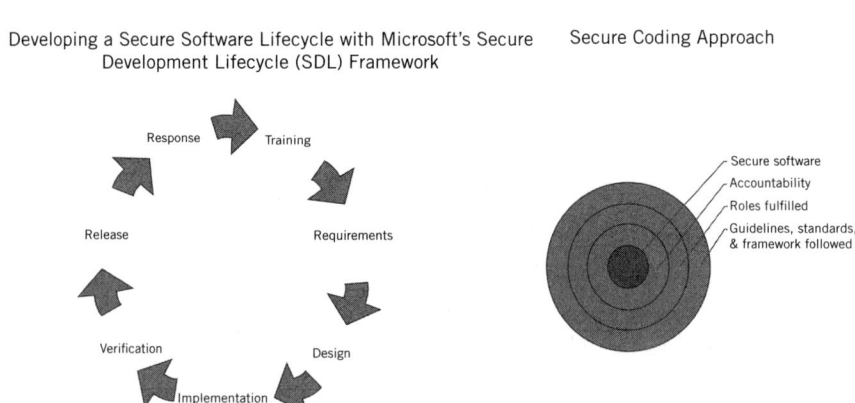

7. **Close** the **browser window**.

8. Using your research, **complete** the following **table** with security in mind from the beginning, as defined by the Microsoft® Security Development Lifecycle (SDL) framework. Specify who will perform the activities in each phase (roles: coder, software tester, Q&A, etc.), and any tools that may be used during the process.

PHASE	ACTIVITIES	ROLES	TOOLS
Requirements			
Design			
Implementation			
Verification			
Release			
Response			
Training			

9. In a new text document, **create** a **Security Development Life Cycle Plan** that includes each of the following elements (you will be responsible for determining what to document in this life cycle based on what you learned in your research):

- Executive Summary
- Table of Contents
- Overview of each phase of software development and the activities that occur within that phase
- Activities and Roles (your answers to step 8 above)
- Summary of Findings (your answers to step 6 above)

For this test scenario, assume that you are the network administrator for Online Goodies, an Internet-based company that provides custom promotional gifts, such as T-shirts, mugs, computer accessories, and office décor items, to its corporate customers. This is an e-commerce site that receives most of its income from online credit card purchases. Repeat customers receive discounts based on the amount of their total annual purchases.

10. **Submit** the **Security Development Life Cycle Plan** to your instructor as a deliverable for this lab.

Evaluation Criteria and Rubrics

The following are the evaluation criteria and rubrics for Lab #10 that students must perform:

1. Was the student able to design a general security life cycle strategy for a Web application based on the software development life cycle (SDLC)? – [**20%**]

2. Was the student able to recognize how automated and manual processes can benefit a security life cycle strategy, mapping recommendations to best practices? – [**20%**]

3. Was the student able to identify the various roles when implementing a security life cycle strategy, and assign these roles to individuals within an organization? – [**20%**]

4. Was the student able to integrate a compliance process into a security life cycle strategy, so that applications that must meet regulatory compliance are up to the standards required? – [**20%**]

5. Was the student able to identify appropriate tools for use in each phase of the software development life cycle for proper implementation of best practice guidelines? – [**20%**]

LAB #10 – ASSESSMENT WORKSHEET

Build a Web Application and Security Development Life Cycle Plan

Course Name and Number:
_____

Student Name:
_____

Instructor Name:
_____

Lab Due Date:
_____

Overview

In this lab, you conducted research into the Microsoft® Security Development Lifecycle (SDL) and the traditional software development life cycle (SDLC). Using that research, you drafted a Security Development Life Cycle Plan for an Internet sales company, Online Goodies, which incorporated checkpoints for proper security testing and penetration testing for Web servers and Web applications.

Lab Assessment Questions & Answers

1. List and briefly describe the steps in the Security Development Lifecycle (SDL).

_____

_____

_____

_____

_____

2. Explain what STRIDE is and specify what the acronym stands for.

_____

_____

_____

_____

3. Explain the use of the g_pFoo-encoded pointer and which step of the SDL covers this function and its proper usage.

_____

_____

_____

_____

4. Why is it necessary for software that follows a strenuous SDL to include a response phase?

_____

_____

_____

_____

5. What are three Microsoft® categories for software code that define requirements for 64-bit compilers, tools, and options?

_____

_____

_____

_____

6. Explain what the Heap Manager Fail Fast Setting will enable on a Microsoft® OS and why it is a recommended security setting. In which Microsoft® OS did this setting become available?

_____

_____

_____

_____

7. Where in the SDL process do Web server, Web application, and penetration testing occur?

_____

_____

_____

_____

_____

8. Which core areas should a training program cover during the SDLC?

_____

_____

_____

_____

9. Explain deprecation as it pertains to SDL or SDLC.

_____

_____

_____

_____

10. Why is the requirements phase so important in both SDL and SDLC?

_____

_____

_____

_____

11. In the SDL, why is it a good idea to create a test plan before the actual code is developed?

_____

_____

_____

_____

12. In which phases in the SDL may a cross-site scripting (XSS) be discovered?

_____

_____

_____

_____

13. In the Microsoft® SDL process, explain the role of an incident-response plan.

_____

_____

_____

_____

14. What is white box testing and at what phase in the SDL should it be introduced?

_____

_____

_____

_____

15. Explain the term _security assurance_. At what phase in the SDL should it be introduced?

_____

_____

_____

_____

_____

_____